New Product Development

New Product Development

Strategies for Supplier Integration

Robert M. Monczka, Ph.D.
Michigan State University

Robert B. Handfield, Ph.D.
North Carolina State University

Thomas V. Scannell, Ph.D.
Western Michigan University

Gary L. Ragatz, Ph.D.
Michigan State University

David J. Frayer, Ph.D.
Michigan State University

ASQ Quality Press
Milwaukee, Wisconsin

New Product Development
R. M. Monczka, R. B. Handfield, T. V. Scannell, G. L. Ragatz, D. J. Frayer

New product development : strategies for supplier integration / Robert M. Monczka ... [et al.].
    p.   cm.
    Includes index.
    ISBN 0-87389-468-5 (alk. paper)
    1. New products—Management. 2. Industrial procurement—Management. I. Monczka, Robert M.
    HF5415.153 .N475 2000
    658.5'75—dc21   99-047759

10 9 8 7 6 5 4 3 2 1

ISBN 0-87389-468-5

Acquisitions Editor: Ken Zielske
Project Editor: Annemieke Koudstaal
Production Administrator: Shawn Dohogne

ASQ Mission: The American Society for Quality advances individual and organizational performance excellence worldwide by providing opportunities for learning, quality improvement, and knowledge exchange.

Attention: Bookstores, Wholesalers, Schools and Corporations:
ASQ Quality Press books, videotapes, audiotapes, and software are available at quantity discounts with bulk purchases for business, educational, or instructional use. For information, please contact ASQ Quality Press at 800-248-1946, or write to ASQ Quality Press, P.O. Box 3005, Milwaukee, WI 53201-3005.

To place orders or to request a free copy of the ASQ Quality Press Publications Catalog, including ASQ membership information, call 800-248-1946. Visit our web site at www.asq.org. or qualitypress.asq.org.

Printed in the United States of America

♾ Printed on acid-free paper

American Society for Quality
ASQ™
Quality Press
611 East Wisconsin Avenue
Milwaukee, Wisconsin 53202
Call toll free 800-248-1946
qualitypress.asq.org

Table of Contents

List of Figures and Tables

Preface

"My company will survive by producing new products, but it will only *thrive* with first-to-market new products."

Executive director, electronics company

Rapid technological change, shortened product life cycles, and increasing global competition make new product development a critical concern for U.S. manufacturers. Research conducted at Michigan State University suggests that over the next five years, competitive pressures will require manufacturers to reduce costs by 5 to 8 percent a year (economics held constant) and continue to improve product quality, while simultaneously reducing time-to-market by 40 to 60 percent.[1] In addition, McKinsey and Company estimates that if a product is late to market by six months, gross profit potential is reduced by 33 percent.[2]

In this competitive environment, suppliers are an increasingly important resource for manufacturers. Across all U.S. manufacturers, purchased materials account for more than 50 percent of the cost of goods sold. In addition, suppliers have a large and direct impact on the elements of cost, quality, technology, speed, and responsiveness of buying companies. More effective integration of suppliers into a firm's product value/supply chain will be a key factor in achieving the improvements necessary to remain competitive. However, very little information is available to guide firms in developing strategies, practices, and implementation approaches to achieve such integration. In the words of one executive, "We have not yet really learned how to fully incorporate suppliers into the design, production, and distribution of our products and leverage their full capabilities through the product value/supply chain."

To address this need, researchers at Michigan State University, with the support of the *National Science Foundation's Transformations to Quality Organizations* program and *The Global Procurement and Supply Chain Benchmarking Initiative at Michigan State*

---

[1]Monczka, Robert M. and Robert J. Trent, "Purchasing and Sourcing Strategy: Trends and Implications," a study published by the Center for Advanced Purchasing Studies, Tempe, Arizona (1995).

[2]McKinsey and Company, 1993.

University, conducted a three-year investigation into the why, what, how, and when of integrating suppliers into new product development. Specifically, the research

1. Develops an explanatory model describing the variables that contribute to the successful integration of suppliers into the new product development process to improve a firm's time-to-market, quality, cost, technology, product features, and delivery/responsiveness performance

2. Identifies and describes the strategies and practices used to integrate suppliers successfully into the new product development process, including

    a. Descriptions of successful strategies/practices

    b. Identification of critical success factors required to achieve supplier integration

    c. Discussion of hard and soft results achieved

    d. Analysis of strategies/practices that were unsuccessful, and why

    e. Future plans to further enhance supplier integration

3. Develops implementation guidelines for firms to follow to enhance supplier integration into their new product development processes

4. Develops case studies and models of supplier integration into the new product development process for use by industry and academia

The research included an extensive literature review, in-depth field research, and electronic and mail surveys. Interdisciplinary industry and academic review teams conducted the research and interpreted results. The research process included

1. Explanatory model development

2. Field research case studies with twenty leading companies worldwide that are successfully integrating suppliers into their new product development processes

3. Research with member companies of The Global Procurement and Supply Chain Benchmarking Initiative at Michigan State University to further develop implementation knowledge based on actual company experiences

4. Explanatory model enhancement based on preliminary field research and Benchmarking Initiative findings

5. Quantitative survey testing of the explanatory model with over 2000 firms worldwide

6. Data analysis using a variety of quantitative and qualitative analysis techniques

7. Development of research findings and report writing

8. Dissemination of research findings

The results will be useful to practicing executives and managers in developing strategies and implementation road maps to be followed in integrating suppliers into the product/value chain to achieve competitive advantage. The models and information developed will enable a focused articulation of an implementation approach that can be shared among different functions within the organization.

In addition, the case studies and overall research results will provide materials that can be used for educational purposes in undergraduate, graduate, and executive education programs throughout the United States to enhance the capabilities of both entry level and seasoned managers.

This book is organized as follows: Chapters 1 and 2 introduce the research and provide an executive overview of the findings. Chapter 3 discusses reengineering strategies and approaches used to establish the climate, culture, and organization needed to improve new product development in general and supplier integration into new product development efforts in particular. Chapters 4 through 6 take a more focused look at the strategic planning process for supplier integration, while Chapters 7 and 8 examine the supplier integration execution process. Chapter 9 examines the barriers and associated solutions related to successful supplier integration. Finally, Chapter 10 provides a summary and conclusion.

ABOUT THE RESEARCH AND FUNDING ORGANIZATIONS

The Global Procurement and Supply Chain Benchmarking Initiative at Michigan State University (MSU), directed by Dr. Robert M. Monczka, began in 1993 as a first-of-its-kind initiative and has evolved into the most comprehensive procurement and supply chain benchmarking operation in the world. The MSU Benchmarking Initiative is a comprehensive third-party benchmarking effort with a worldwide impact on manufacturing and service companies. Critical strategic benchmarking information is collected, analyzed, and disseminated to all participating companies through user-friendly printed reports and electronically via the World Wide Web. A sample of benchmarking initiatives includes strategic supplier alliances, supplier integration into new product/process/service development, insourcing/outsourcing strategies in an integrated supply chain, supplier development and quality management, procurement and supply chain performance measurement, procurement and supply chain globalization strategies, strategic cost management throughout the supply chain, and information systems and technology.

The National Science Foundation's Transformations to Quality Organizations program supports interdisciplinary or multidisciplinary research on quality in organizations. Research supported by this program is based on partnerships between researchers and firms or other organizations. The objectives are to develop or improve concepts, theories, and methodologies for better managing transformations to quality organizations, and to encourage the development of new tools and processes leading to quality improvements in organizations.

Chapter 1

The New Product Development Process in the Context of Supply Chain Management Strategy

"With all the downsizing, I just don't have the internal resources or skill base to design the whole product. Our suppliers must now step to the plate with full service capabilities for us to remain competitive."

Engineering manager, automotive firm

INTRODUCTION AND OBJECTIVES

Firms are facing increasing global competition and markets that demand more frequent innovation and higher quality products and services. The challenge is to be the most customer-focused, responsive, reliable, and cost-effective provider of value through either one or both of two primary value streams: *value delivery* or *value creation*. As Figure 1.1 suggests, value delivery emphasizes order fulfillment flows of materials, products, and services through sourcing, production/operations, and distribution to end customers. Value creation, on the other hand, emphasizes new product/process/service development (hereafter referred to collectively as *NPD*) activities that identify and package customer needs and wants in the form of new products or services. Both value streams require management and involvement of the supply chain to optimize final customer value.

This book is intended for firms that are looking for ways to improve their *value creation* processes. Many firms are looking for ways to decrease NPD cycle time, improve product or service quality and features, and significantly reduce costs. Further, many NPD managers are attempting to meet these objectives with "lean" organizations. Whether companies have become lean through a strategic focus on core competencies or as a result of mandated downsizing, the bottom line is that many NPD managers have fewer internal resources to utilize in NPD efforts.

1

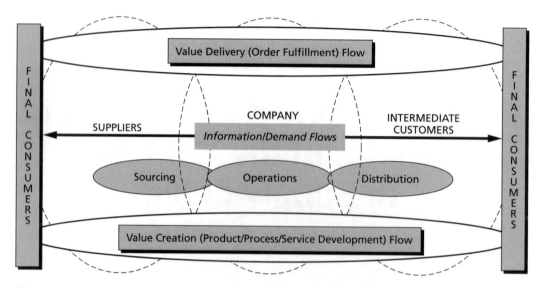

Figure 1.1. Providing value through integrated supply chain management.

To support their objectives, many companies are involving suppliers earlier in the design and development process to gain competitive advantage. Such supplier involvement ranges from simple consultation on design ideas to making suppliers fully responsible for the design of components, systems, processes, or services. The result is often better product design and a product that is brought to market faster at a lower cost with greater quality.

Over the past three years, a research team from The Global Procurement and Supply Chain Benchmarking Initiative at Michigan State University (MSU) has been studying strategies and best practices for integrating suppliers into NPD efforts. An initial benchmarking survey was conducted of the member companies of the MSU Benchmarking Initiative. That survey was followed by in-depth field interviews with 20 leading-edge companies and a second, larger-scale mail survey of companies worldwide. These latter two data collection efforts were partially funded by the National Science Foundation under its Transformations to Quality Organizations program.

Results of the worldwide mail survey show that the 124 responding companies achieved significant improvements in NPD results when suppliers participated, compared to results for similar NPD projects in which suppliers were *not* involved (see Table 1.1). These results illustrate the potential benefits of involving suppliers in new product development efforts, and an important competitive advantage for companies that can manage this integration successfully.

Despite these significant improvements, the survey also revealed that relatively little is known about how to best integrate suppliers into NPD. As one manager noted, "Our suppliers are our greatest *untapped* resource. We don't know how to effectively and equitably integrate them into our business processes." This suggests that there is a real managerial need to better understand the structures, strategies, and processes that drive effective supplier integration. Further, it points to the need for development of new learning tools and

Table 1.1. Overall performance improvements achieved through supplier integration.*

Performance Dimension	Median % Improvement	Range**
Purchased Material Cost (n = 71)***	15.0%	2.6%–50.0%
Purchased Material Quality (n = 52)	20.0%	2.0%–50.0%
Development Time (n = 65)	20.0%	5.0%–50.0%
Development Cost (n = 54)	15.0%	−1.0%–50.0%
Functionality/Features/Technology (n = 53)	10.0%	5.0%–50.0%
Product Manufacturing Cost (n = 49)	10.0%	0.0%–30.0%

*Compared to similar projects in which a supplier was not integrated.
**80% of the companies' responses fall in this range; top and bottom 10% omitted.
***Not all companies reported results on all dimensions.

materials to promote increased emphasis on NPD strategies in the classroom and executive education programs. This book therefore

1. Develops an explanatory model describing the factors that contribute to the successful integration of suppliers into the NPD process to improve a firm's time-to-market, quality, cost, technology, product features, and delivery/responsiveness performance

2. Identifies and describes the strategies and practices used to integrate suppliers successfully into the new product development process, including

   a. Descriptions of successful strategies/practices

   b. Identification of critical success factors required to achieve supplier integration

   c. Discussion of hard and soft results achieved

   d. Analysis of strategies/practices that were unsuccessful

   e. Future plans to further enhance supplier integration

3. Develops implementation guidelines to enhance supplier integration into new product development processes

4. Develops case studies and models of supplier integration into the new product development process for use by industry and academia

The two primary supplier integration process models developed from the research are presented in the following figures. Figure 1.2 identifies the key stages in the supplier integration strategic planning process, while Figure 1.3 presents the supplier integration execution process.

These models indicate that for long-term competitive advantage, supplier integration must be driven from the top down, with decision-making authority and accountability assigned at the proper organizational level. An executive summary of these models is presented in Chapter 2. Chapter 3 is a discussion of the NPD process in general and the increasing role of suppliers in NPD. Detailed discussion of these models follows. We

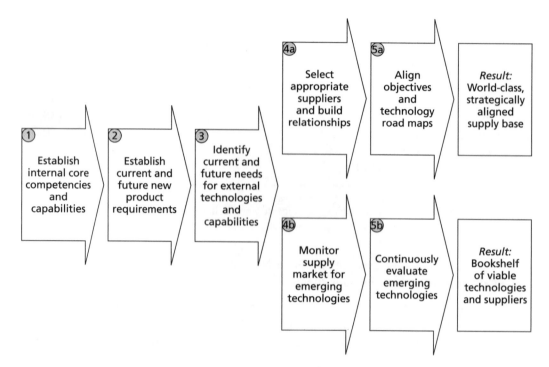

Figure 1.2. Supplier integration strategic planning process.

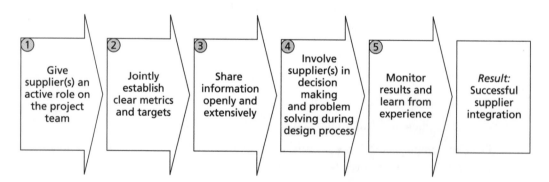

Figure 1.3. Supplier integration execution process.

address some of the barriers to effective supplier integration in Chapter 9, and how companies are managing to overcome these barriers. Finally, Chapter 10 provides an overall summary and conclusion.

THE NEW PRODUCT DEVELOPMENT PROCESS

The new product development process is a series of interdependent and often overlapping stages during which a new product (or process or service) is brought from the idea stage

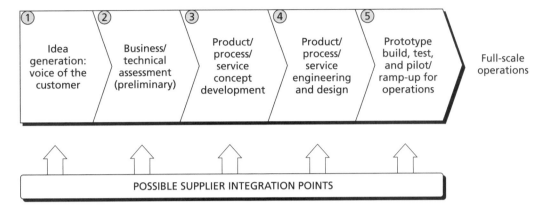

Figure 1.4. The new product development process.

to readiness for full-scale production or operation. As the product concept moves through these stages, the idea is refined and evaluated for business and technical feasibility; the design is firmed up; prototyping and testing are done; the design is finalized; and preparations for full-scale operations such as tooling, layout, and equipment are finalized. During this process, cost, performance, timing, quality, and other problems develop, resulting in trade-offs and changes in the design. The design may be modified numerous times before it is finalized.

External suppliers provide materials and services that comprise a majority of the cost of many new products. In addition, suppliers may provide innovative or freshened product or process technologies that are critical to the development effort. The supplier may have greater knowledge or expertise regarding these technologies than the buying company. Supplier input and/or the active involvement of suppliers may be sought at any point in the development process (see Figure 1.4).

While the concept and design engineering phases of new product development incur a relatively small portion of total product development costs, these two activities can commit or "lock in" as much as 80 percent of the total cost of the product. Decisions made early in the design process have a significant impact on product quality, cycle time, and cost. As the development process continues, it becomes increasingly difficult and costly to make design changes (see Figure 1.5).

It is crucial, then, for firms to bring to bear as much product, process, and technical expertise as possible early in the development process. Companies whose development plans are well-aligned with those of their key suppliers can harness the resource not only to minimize design and development cycle times while increasing value, but also to minimize the number, complexity, and cost of design changes throughout the life of the product. This can be accomplished through (1) use of preestablished technology development plans; (2) use of products and processes developed in advance of NPD efforts (bookshelf technologies); and (3) concurrent development and testing of assemblies, subassemblies, and piece parts, for example.

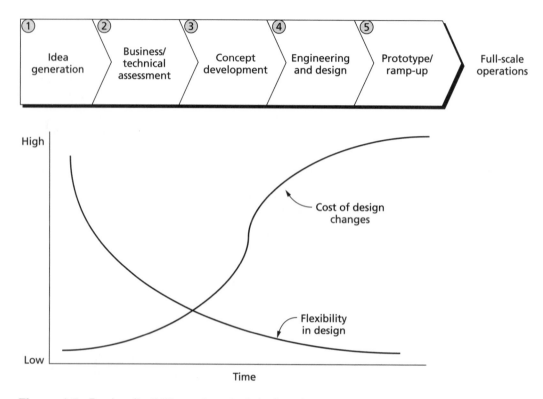

Figure 1.5. Design flexibility and cost of design changes.

INCREASING ROLE AND IMPACT OF SUPPLIERS

While supplier input can be beneficial at any stage in the development process, earlier involvement appears to offer greater advantages. Among the companies responding to our survey, those who integrated suppliers earlier in the new product development process reported larger improvements in product cost, quality, development time, development cost, and functionality/features/technology (see Table 1.2).

The companies in our sample, which represent a wide range of industries, recognize the potential benefits of integrating suppliers early in the development process, and a large majority indicate that this type of involvement will be expanding in the future. A significant majority also said that they believe suppliers will be involved in the development process earlier in future NPD efforts (see Figure 1.6).

Of course, not all suppliers need to be integrated early in the design process, nor do they need to have the same level of involvement. Figure 1.7 shows a spectrum of ways suppliers may be integrated, ranging from no integration to "black-box" integration. The no-integration situation represents a traditional "make-to-print" or "provide the service the customer asks for" role for the supplier. This is in stark contrast to black-box integration, where the supplier has primary responsibility for the design of a component, system, process, or service, typically working from general performance requirements either

Table 1.2. Median performance improvement by stage of first integration of supplier.*

| | *Stage of First Integration* | | |
Performance Dimension	Early (Stage 1 or 2)	Middle (Stage 3)	Late (Stage 4 or 5)
Purchased Material Cost	20.0%	15.0%	10.0%
Purchased Material Quality	20.0%	15.0%	15.0%
Development Time	20.0%	20.0%	10.0%
Development Cost	20.0%	10.0%	10.0%
Functionality/Features/Technology	20.0%	10.0%	10.0%
Product Manufacturing Cost	10.0%	12.0%	10.0%

*Compared to similar projects in which a supplier was not integrated.

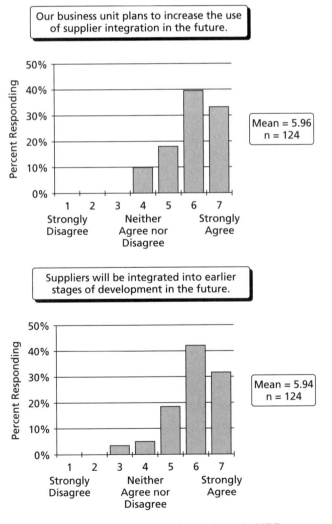

Figure 1.6. Increased and earlier integration of suppliers in NPD.

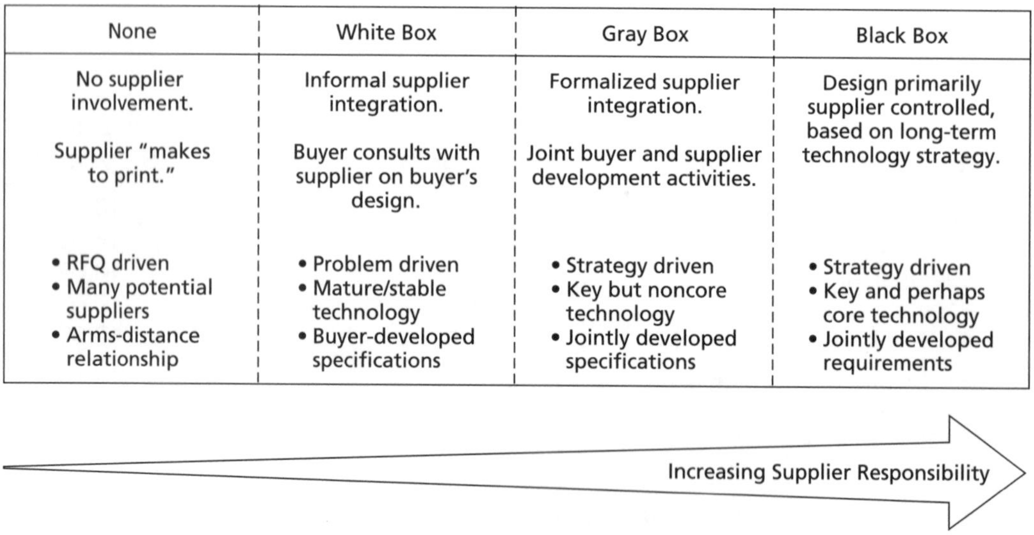

None	White Box	Gray Box	Black Box
No supplier involvement.	Informal supplier integration.	Formalized supplier integration.	Design primarily supplier controlled, based on long-term technology strategy.
Supplier "makes to print."	Buyer consults with supplier on buyer's design.	Joint buyer and supplier development activities.	
• RFQ driven • Many potential suppliers • Arms-distance relationship	• Problem driven • Mature/stable technology • Buyer-developed specifications	• Strategy driven • Key but noncore technology • Jointly developed specifications	• Strategy driven • Key and perhaps core technology • Jointly developed requirements

Increasing Supplier Responsibility

Figure 1.7. Spectrum of supplier integration.

Table 1.3.   Median performance improvement by level of integration.*

	Level of Integration	
Performance Dimension	**Gray Box**	**Black Box**
Purchased Material Cost	15.0%	20.0%
Purchased Material Quality	15.0%	20.0%
Development Time	20.0%	20.0%
Development Cost	10.0%	20.0%
Functionality/Features/Technology	10.0%	12.5%
Product Manufacturing Cost	10.0%	20.0%

*Compared to similar projects in which a supplier was not integrated.

provided by or developed with the buying company. Of course, even in the case of black-box integration, the buying company retains ultimate approval authority for the design.

Consistent with the finding of greater benefits through earlier supplier involvement, survey results show that companies that give suppliers greater responsibility in the new product development process tend to achieve greater benefits from the supplier integration (see Table 1.3). The companies reporting on examples of black-box integration reported larger average improvements in production cost, quality, and development cost than the companies reporting on "gray-box" integration efforts. The survey did not address "white-box" integration.

Along with depth of involvement, related factors such as dollar value of the supplied item, design complexity, and newness of the technology will determine the appropriate timing of supplier involvement (see Figure 1.8). The firms in our study that were most suc-

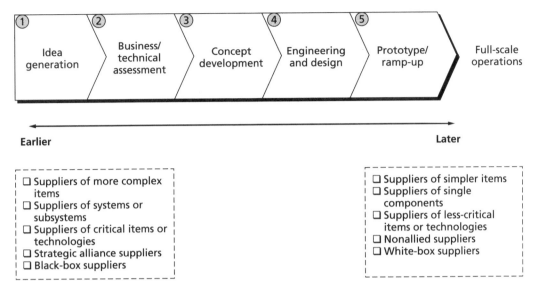

Figure 1.8. Timing of supplier integration.

cessful at supplier integration used a systematic approach that was formalized and integrated into company processes to determine when to integrate a supplier.

CONCLUSION

The case for early integration of suppliers in the new product development process is compelling, but it is important to recognize that supplier integration is a process that must be managed properly to achieve maximum impact. The greatest barriers to effective supplier integration, as perceived by respondents, were

- Unwillingness of buying company technical staff to relinquish design or technology development responsibilities (the "not invented here" syndrome)

- Supplier concern over protecting proprietary cost information

- Buying company concern over protecting proprietary cost information

- The time required to identify and integrate a supplier

- Buying company concern over protecting proprietary technology

- The lack of processes for integrating suppliers

Our field research has revealed a number of valuable strategies and practices for overcoming some of these barriers and effectively managing supplier integration into new product development. Successful companies apply these solutions at three levels: (1) the policy level, where the structure of the new product development process is defined and reengineered; (2) the strategic planning level; and (3) the execution level. An executive review of the key strategies and processes at each of these levels is presented in Chapter 2.

Chapter 2

Executive Review

"Two years ago, integrating suppliers into new product development was putting the cart before the horse. We changed our structures, policies and practices, adopted new tools, and effectively reengineered our organizational culture before aggressively developing and implementing a supplier integration strategy. Now, not only is the cart behind the horse, but we have some real thoroughbreds leading the way."

Supply chain manager, automotive firm

INTRODUCTION AND OBJECTIVES

Supplier integration into NPD processes cuts across internal functions as well as external supplier and customer organizations. Extensively spanning processes such as these requires a foundation on which specific strategies and processes are coordinated, built, and sustained. This chapter provides an executive overview of research findings by summarizing the key strategies and processes for reengineering the NPD process, developing supplier integration into NPD strategy, and implementing the strategy.

REENGINEERING THE NEW PRODUCT DEVELOPMENT PROCESS

In order for supplier integration to be successful in new product development, the new product development process must support an active role for suppliers, customers, and all internal functions and processes. Such a new product development process should be characterized by the attributes shown in Table 2.1.

The new product development processes at many of the firms we studied were reengineered during the 1990s and now undergo regular review to further improve the processes and reduce product development time. We found a number of key enabling tools and practices being used to help improve the effectiveness of the reengineered NPD system (see Table 2.2).

Table 2.3 contrasts several key strategic elements of traditional and reengineered new product development processes. These elements focus on making the most effective use of the resources and competencies of both the buyer and supplier.

Table 2.1. New product development attributes.

- Decisions guided by the firm's overall business strategy/priorities
- Policy that dictates what is to be done
- Decisions guided by an established strategic insourcing/outsourcing process for NPD actvities
- Simple new product development process structure that is clear and can be followed by all functions and project team members, as well as all suppliers involved in the process
- A careful assessment of customer/user needs and requirements
- A clearly defined, early role for procurement and suppliers

Table 2.2. New product development enabling tools and practices.

- Application of project management tools
- Risk assessment
- Activity-based costing
- Common hardware and software
- Rapid and concurrent development processes—prototypes and tools
- Choice of bookshelf suppliers and technology
- Sharing of technology road maps between firms
- Reduction of product portfolios
- Common building blocks for products/processes/services
- Use of industry standard materials, products, and processes
- Part/process standardization
- Empowered project managers who can "kill" projects
- Common goals, measurements, rewards
- Cross-functional teams with a customer focus

Table 2.3. Structuring the new product development process: key strategic elements.

Traditional Structure	Reengineered Structure
No critical review/analysis of the current new product development process for continuous improvement opportunities	Culture that encourages and supports change not just for the sake of change, but for making continuous improvement even when there is no apparent problem
Internal design and development of all key components, subsystems, and systems	Focus on core technology development, allowing supplier integration into noncore, yet critical, systems
Emphasis strictly on negotiating skills in the purchasing organization	Development of technical competence in the purchasing organization
Limited or no support for supplier development	Company dedicated resources to develop key suppliers' capabilities for integration into new product development
Limited long-term information-sharing with suppliers	Alignment of key suppliers' long-term goals and technology plans with the buying company's long-term needs

(continued)

- Blind commitment to see the development effort to completion once the process has reached a certain point (e.g., dollars spent)
- No strategic supplier alliances to identify customer requirements and develop new products ideas

- Stage gates at each step in the development process, which yield a "go or no-go" decision
- Formation of strategic alliances, joint identification of customer requirements, and development of product concepts

---

CASE EXAMPLE

Two Bosses + Two Processes = One Objective

The matrix organization (see Figure 2.1) adopted by one company we examined illustrates a reengineered new product development process. Key functional groups are matrixed with the company's product lines, facilitating the involvement of functional competency groups in the product development process. The structure permits personnel within each functional group to develop expertise in a specific product line, while promoting transfer of knowledge across product lines.

The company has two key strategies with respect to procurement and the suppliers' roles in new product development. The company is attempting to:

- Increase supplier responsibility for design and development activities

- Increase supplier responsibility for product modules or systems rather than individual components

To facilitate this expanded role for suppliers and remove the supplier selection decision from the critical path for new product development, the company has developed

(continued)

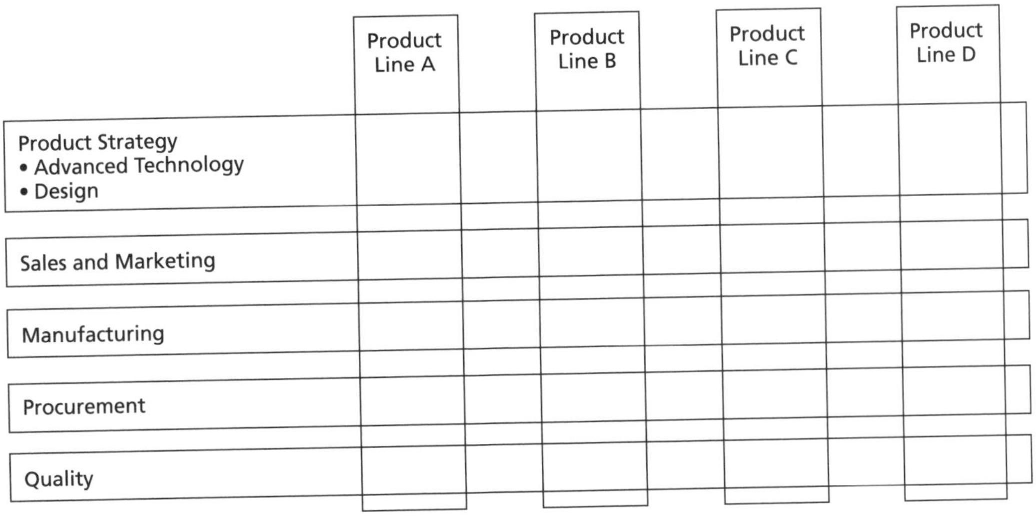

	Product Line A		Product Line B		Product Line C		Product Line D	
Product Strategy • Advanced Technology • Design								
Sales and Marketing								
Manufacturing								
Procurement								
Quality								

Figure 2.1. Matrixed new product development organization.

two strategic processes for managing supplier integration into new product development: early supplier involvement and early sourcing. Early supplier involvement takes place before any design activity starts. At this point, the company focuses on evaluating different technologies and assessing their feasibility with respect to broad cost targets. Early sourcing comes later, as the company's internal design activity begins. At this point, the company formally commits its business to a specific supplier, and the supplier's design work commences. These processes are standardized across the company's product lines and help facilitate the transfer of knowledge regarding new technologies and supply base capabilities between the procurement function and product line management.

CASE EXAMPLE

Double Team, Triple Team, Quadruple Team

A second company we studied defined its overall new product development process in terms of six overlapping processes (similar to the NPD process model presented in Chapter 1):

- Planning and program definition
- Product design and development
- Process design and development
- Product and process verification
- Production
- Feedback, assessment, and corrective action

This process is implemented through a hierarchical structure of cross-functional teams (see Figure 2.2). Cross-functional teams include representatives from product

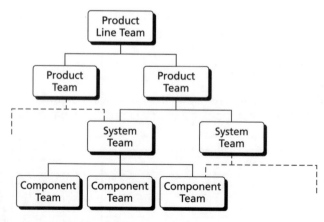

Figure 2.2. Hierarchical cross-functional team structure.

planning, product design, engineering, advanced manufacturing, manufacturing, procurement, finance, sales and marketing, and the supply base, as needed. The product line team, which is generally composed of high-level managers from all functional areas, largely determines how resources will be allocated to product teams. Product teams then determine how best to utilize and manage the allocated resources. The product is divided into its major systems and assemblies, and system teams are created and assigned overall responsibility for their system. This process continues until the lowest logical level of input is determined. Responsibilities and appropriate level of decision making are assigned at each level by the product team. While such a structure is increasingly common, this company formally establishes—prior to team development—who should be considered for team membership and requires justification for not including internal functions or suppliers on the core team.

Critical to effective long-term change is establishing the foundation to support change. For driving increased and earlier involvement of suppliers into NPD, alignment of the company's organizational strategy/structure, NPD strategy/processes, and purchasing/supply chain management strategy/processes is required. Such internal alignment establishes and enables the key processes and strategies shown in Table 2.4.

NPD teams must be empowered to make important decisions consistent with their level of responsibility. These decisions include managing the day-to-day activities of the project, working out business and technical issues, and selecting suppliers, for example. These teams may work jointly with suppliers to develop the technical and business expectations of each party. The teams also should develop risk management strategies and understand the consequences of failure to perform. Such structures, policies, and processes enable supplier integration in strategic planning and execution.

Table 2.4. Internal strategy alignment: key to long-term competitiveness.

- Culture that encourages and supports change not just for the sake of change, but for making continuous improvement even when there is no apparent problem
- Focus on core technology development, allowing supplier integration into noncore, yet critical, systems
- Development of technical competence in the purchasing organization
- Company dedicated resources to develop key suppliers' capabilities for integration into new product development
- Alignment of key suppliers' long-term goals and technology plans with the buying company's long-term needs
- Stage gates at each step in the NPD process which yield a "go or no-go" decision
- Formation of strategic alliances, joint identification of customer requirements, and development of product concepts

SUPPLIER INTEGRATION: STRATEGIC PLANNING PROCESS

In the companies that are benefiting most from supplier integration into new product development, supplier integration is a strategic initiative that is undertaken as part of the company's overall competitive strategy. The reasons for approaching supplier integration from a strategic perspective are to insure that the company makes the best competitive use of its internal core competencies, and to insure that the company has external access to the capabilities and technologies that will properly complement its internal core competencies over the long term.

To achieve these objectives, a company must put in place systematic processes for determining its current and future needs for external capabilities and technologies, for building a world-class supply base that will help meet those needs, and for developing a "bookshelf" of current and emerging technologies that will become available to meet future requirements, as well as suppliers for those technologies. Based on our study of best practices, we have developed a process (see Figure 2.3) to help guide organizations in establishing supplier integration strategies.

Steps 1, 2, 3—Determining Current and Future Needs

A key to strategic planning for supplier integration is establishing those technologies and capabilities the company will seek from outside sources and those it will develop internally. Many new products require application of a wide variety of product and process technologies. No single company is likely to have sufficient technological expertise to

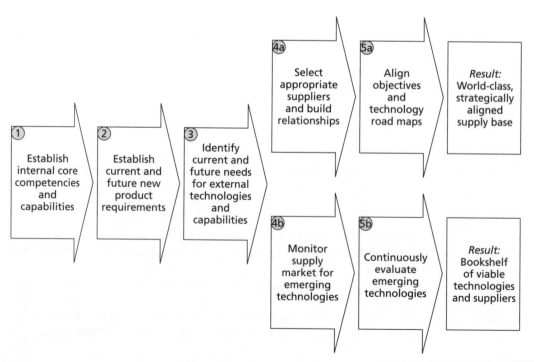

Figure 2.3. Supplier integration strategic planning process.

internalize all design and production effectively. In fact, trying to do everything in-house may lead to a competitive disadvantage. Each company needs to define and focus on doing what is most critical to its competitive success, what it is best equipped to do, and perhaps most importantly what it is most profitable to do, then rely on external sources to carry out other processes.

A careful comparison of internal core competencies, capabilities, and capacity with current and projected future new product requirements will define the required objectives in terms of an aligned supply base. Many companies find high-level cross-functional teams an effective tool for making this decision. Representatives from design, manufacturing, procurement, project team management, and quality develop a strategy that is aligned with the company's overall strategic priorities and market requirements. A systematic insourcing/ outsourcing process is required and should include analysis of competitive market position, cost, quality, technology, and responsiveness/delivery, all within the strategic plan of the firm. Ultimately, this is a high-level decision that filters down to the cross-functional team level and to commodity teams.

CASE EXAMPLE

Corporate Strategy

One company classifies every item that goes into its product as "core," "leveraged," or "build to print" (see Figure 2.4). Items that differentiate the company's products in the market and that have high dollar value or technical complexity are labeled "core." The company retains all design and development responsibility for core items, though on occasion they may form a strategic alliance with a supplier that has unique capabilities or expertise. Leveraged items are either key market differentiators or high-dollar-value items that require technical expertise outside of the company's current competency/ capability. For leveraged items, the company will have varying levels of control on design and development, but will outsource the majority of production. Build-to-print

(continued)

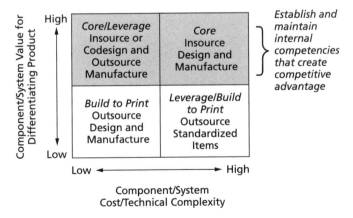

Figure 2.4. Corporate strategy.

items are those with low differentiating value. Build to print in this case also includes build to requirements (that is, outsource design and manufacture) when the item has low differentiating value and low dollar value, for example. Build to print may also include high-dollar-value items when the company currently has no supplier with full design capability.

Steps 4a, 5a—Developing a Well-Aligned World-Class Supply Base

Most companies expect a supplier who is involved in the design process to also supply at least a portion of the volume production requirements for the item, so supplier selection criteria relevant for any sourcing decision will be relevant here as well. There are likely to be additional criteria, however, specific to considering a supplier for integration into a NPD effort. Based on the companies we interviewed, the extra criteria included items such as those listed in Table 2.5.

The relative importance of these specific criteria varies from company to company and from project to project. The fundamental objective is to achieve alignment between the buying company's needs and the supplier's capabilities both from a technical standpoint and a cultural/behavioral standpoint.

Concern with alignment is not a short-term issue. The supplier's future capabilities will be as important as, if not more important than, its current capabilities, and achieving alignment is a continuous process that both companies will have to work at over time. The companies who responded to our survey identified their most effective practices for identifying, developing, and maintaining a capable, well-aligned supply base (see Table 2.6).

For any supplier integration effort to be successful, both organizations must be committed to the relationship. Supplier involvement in a product development effort is a new and uncomfortable type of relationship for many companies. Without a solid commitment in both organizations, the communication and sharing of information and resources necessary to make the relationship work will probably not occur. One of the keys to achieving necessary commitment is having top management demonstrate support within both

Table 2.5.   Additional selection criteria for full-service suppliers.

- Design and engineering capability
- Willingness to be involved in the design effort
- Ability to meet the schedule for the development effort
- Research and development capability and technology leadership
- Willingness to share cost and technology information
- Cultural compatibility with the buying company
- Willingness to colocate design/engineering personnel
- Sufficient resources to participate over the entire design process
- Ability to reach agreement on risk sharing, intellectual property rights, confidentiality, and nondisclosure issues

companies on a regular basis. Many of the companies studied coordinated their supplier integration efforts at the highest levels of the two organizations.

Another important element in gaining commitment to the relationship is ensuring that both parties understand the potential benefits/rewards of the relationship, both short-term and long-term. Some firms use formalized risk/reward sharing agreements to explicitly identify what each party can expect from the relationship. This kind of agreement can be particularly useful when a supplier is to be involved in the earlier stages of the development effort. It is equally important that the two companies develop and agree to mutual goals and performance metrics, both in the short and long term.

CASE EXAMPLE

Process Alliance

One of the companies we studied has achieved significant cost savings and manufacturing process improvements through a strategic alliance relationship with a supplier of a key element of its process technology. The company and its supplier hold periodic high-level meetings at which they discuss their respective technology plans. The buying company provides information about anticipated developments in its product lines and their possible implications for its process technology requirements. The supplier provides information about new process technology developments it is pursuing. This level of information sharing requires a high level of initial trust between the parties as well as continuous strengthening of the trust through performance over time.

The buying company may alter its product plans based on information about process technology developments, and the supplier may adjust its development efforts to focus on developments that are a higher priority to the buying company. This approach helps to keep the companies better aligned, and both companies benefit. The buying company has greater assurance that needed process technology will be available, and the supplier has greater assurance that there will be a market for the technologies it is developing.

Table 2.6. Key practices to secure a powerful supply base for NPD.

- Sharing future product plans with key suppliers
- Sharing technology road maps with key suppliers
- Requesting/requiring that key suppliers share their future technology road maps with the buying company
- Giving suppliers access to the buying company to demonstrate new technologies
- Creating a separate organizational group in the buying company responsible for advanced technology development
- Entering into joint technology development with suppliers
- Developing longer-term relationships/alliances with suppliers
- Using continuous improvement targets in agreements with suppliers

---

The Standard Bearer

One of the high-tech companies we examined shares its technology road maps regularly with the supplier of one of its critical product systems, which is an industry-standard item. Through discussions and long-term planning with the supplier's designers, the company has been able to influence the features included in the industry standard. By driving the leading edge of the standard, the company is best able to plan its own product platforms and is often first to market with new product introductions—a key competitive advantage in this industry.

Steps 4b, 5b—Developing a Bookshelf of Viable Technologies and Suppliers

Along with developing a well-aligned world-class supply base, many companies attempt to manage and obtain the best technologies for application by developing a bookshelf of current and emerging technologies and suppliers of those technologies. These companies monitor the development of new technologies and, for those that appear to have promising applications, manage their introduction in new product applications so as to balance the benefits of "first mover" status with the risks of the technology. The objective is to maintain a selection of promising and accessible technologies and suppliers on the bookshelf, ready for use when the company wants to apply them in a new product application. The company must understand, influence, and possibly manage the development time of technologies so that they will be available when needed (see Figure 2.5).

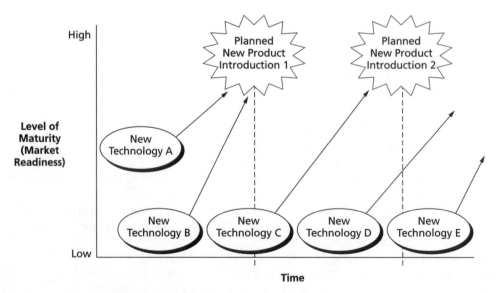

Figure 2.5. Managing product and technology development.

CASE EXAMPLE

Window of Technology

One of the companies studied, which uses supplier-provided technologies extensively in its new products, has established an Advanced Technology Group that is charged with managing the development and adoption of new technologies for the company's products. The Advanced Technology Group monitors the supply market for new technologies and also takes a proactive role in developing technologies called for by the company's product line teams. In some cases, the Advanced Technology Group will undertake development itself, and in other cases, it will pursue suppliers to develop the technology.

This company has also implemented what it calls a "window of technology" program to help improve its access to new or developing technologies. The program, managed by the Advanced Technology Group, provides a single point of contact in the company for a supplier who wants to propose a new technology or new product idea to the company. The supplier's idea gets a fair hearing, but the information is handled confidentially by the Advanced Technology Group, so the idea is protected. If the company is interested in the idea, it may commit to specific volume with the supplier, or it may work with the supplier to develop the technology further.

CASE EXAMPLE

Technology Queue

Another company has an ongoing partnership with a supplier for development of new technologies that leverage the core competencies of each firm. Periodic meetings are held to discuss ideas for advanced technology development projects and to jointly select a set of future projects to pursue, based on applications potential, resources required, and so on. The companies try to have a set number of projects under way at all times. At least one project is under way in each of three categories: "blue-sky" technologies, "rapidly emerging" technologies, and "maturing" technologies. As one project is completed or terminated, the firms select a replacement from the queue.

SUPPLIER INTEGRATION: EXECUTION PROCESS

In addition to having an effective strategic plan, successful supplier integration requires each individual implementation effort to be managed effectively. The purpose of the execution process is to ensure that key required actions are followed during the NPD project. Adhering to these steps fully ensures that the buying company maximizes the value of the supplier's knowledge and capability. Key issues in the execution process focus on enhancing the quality of the supplier's participation in the design process. A model execution process for supplier integration is illustrated in Figure 2.6.

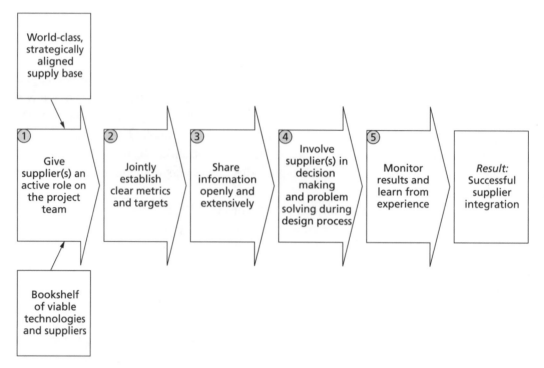

Figure 2.6. Supplier integration execution process.

Step 1—Give Supplier(s) an Active Role

The companies experiencing the greatest success with supplier integration into new product development are those that make the supplier an active participant on the project team. Our findings suggest that the extent of the supplier's participation was the factor most strongly associated with the achievement of project goals. Supplier representatives do not necessarily have to be present at every NPD team meeting, but the suppliers must be kept apprised of and must participate in decisions that are relevant to their involvement. Generally, the greater the complexity of the development effort and the more that is expected of the supplier, the greater the level of supplier participation. Increased participation requires increasing levels of trust as more and potentially proprietary information is transferred between parties.

At times, it may be beneficial to physically colocate supplier and buying company personnel. This allows face-to-face interaction and facilitates problem solving. Companies using colocation felt strongly that they were able to share information more effectively with suppliers who were colocated. Colocation was used by only 58 percent of the companies in our research, but was used more frequently (about 75 percent of the time) for more complex development efforts, such as the design of product systems or subsystems. In these efforts, we found that the use of colocation was positively associated with goal achievement.

We found a variety of models of colocation. One company operates what it calls a "guest engineer" program, through which it invites key suppliers to place an engineer in the buying company's facility for two to three weeks in the very early stages of product development. During this period, the firms develop product/design requirements specifications and assign responsibilities for development. A different buying company colocates its personnel and the supplier's personnel at a neutral site due to union rules. The result is the same—a focused and closely integrated team that works together throughout the duration or just during critical stages of the development project.

CASE EXAMPLE

Protecting the Core

One high-tech company has a core team for each product development project and forms subteams to work on each of the major components or systems of the product. The core team is composed of internal company personnel only, including engineering/design, manufacturing engineering, manufacturing planning, quality assurance, and procurement. Suppliers participate as members of or even lead the subteams for the product system they are involved with. This gives the suppliers an active role, but still maintains a high level of confidentiality for the overall project.

Step 2—Establish Clear Metrics and Targets

Clearly defined and understood metrics and targets are important to the success of almost any project. They are particularly critical when two or more organizations are working jointly on a NPD effort. Clearly defined and agreed-to targets give the parties a common direction and serve as a basis for evaluating progress, making trade-offs, and resolving conflicts. Our research shows that clarity of metrics and targets is particularly important when the two companies have limited experience working together.

Most of the companies we studied have in place market-driven target costing systems that start by establishing an overall maximum target cost for a new product, based on market requirements. The overall target cost is then allocated across major product systems and components. Supplier input is often sought regarding these more detailed-level targets. Suppliers, because of their technical knowledge or expertise, may have valuable information about what are achievable goals and what trade-offs might be involved in achieving particular goals. The buying company will have the ultimate authority in goal-setting, but the supplier's involvement can help in setting goals that are aggressive but reasonable, and also in assuring the supplier's buy-in to the goals.

Targets are not limited to cost, but often include product performance characteristics (such as weight, size, speed) and project performance measures (such as development time). The key issue is that the product development effort must be target-driven. Success demands well-defined and shared targets.

Step 3—Share Information Openly and Extensively

At a basic level, supplier integration into new product development provides benefits because it facilitates better decision making and problem resolution at an earlier stage in the development process. This requires significant communication between the buying and supplying companies during the process, and also requires that significant amounts of information be shared by the companies.

Information on customer requirements, costs, and technology are important for target-setting as well as for decision making and problem resolution during the design effort. As mentioned previously, sharing of technology road-map information can be helpful in achieving longer-term alignment between the organizations.

The ability of design and engineering personnel in two organizations to communicate directly is critical. If the communication process is cumbersome, it discourages communication and slows down the decision-making process. To avoid potential problems with direct communication channels, guidelines for appropriate—and inappropriate—communications need to be established, communicated, and adhered to.

A major barrier to open communication and information sharing for many companies is a concern over disclosure of proprietary information. This can be alleviated to some extent by the use of formal confidentiality or nondisclosure agreements. Use of this kind of agreement is especially valuable when a supplier is being integrated into the earliest stages of the product development process.

CASE EXAMPLE

Progressively Confidential

One company uses two types of confidentiality agreements when working with suppliers on NPD. The first is a broad, general agreement used early in any discussions with a supplier, which commits both companies to nondisclosure of information. As work progresses, a more detailed agreement specific to the particular product or technology being discussed is prepared. Ownership of jointly developed technologies is clearly established in advance, as well as production work commitments.

Confidentiality and nondisclosure agreements can positively influence information sharing, but at some level, sharing must be based on trust between the parties. Solid buy-in and commitment of top management in both firms can help establish an environment of trust, but ultimately the only way to firmly establish a trusting relationship is to perform over time and *earn* the trust of the other party. Many of the companies participating in this research indicated that their willingness to share information with a supplier was a function of their familiarity and past involvement with the supplier. The relationship often needs to be instigated by the buying company by "breaking the ice" and approaching the supplier in an open manner.

Electronic linkages between the companies can also facilitate communication and information sharing. Many companies find the ability to share designs via a common computer-aided design (CAD) system to be very helpful, permitting a type of virtual colocation. Some problems exist however, due to the variety of CAD system standards that are available. Key tools that facilitate interfirm communication are listed in Table 2.7.

Table 2.7. Tools that facilitate interfirm communication.

* Periodic face-to-face meetings
* Point-to-point interfirm communication between functional personnel
* Joint teleconferences
* Temporary colocation at either company or at a neutral site
* E-mail, EDI, fax, and linked CAD/CAM systems

Step 4—Involve Suppliers in Decision Making and Problem Solving During Design

Our findings indicate that supplier involvement on a new product development team led to better decisions and faster problem resolution during the design process. One company, which worked with a supplier on the design of several different components of a new product, described how the supplier was able to suggest a way to meet overall product targets by making a weight/cost trade-off involving several different components on which the supplier was working. Colocation, as mentioned earlier, is valued primarily for its effect on the companies' ability to address design problems quickly as they arise in the design process. Companies who used colocation found it to be extremely effective for problem solving during design, ramp-up, and full volume operations.

Step 5—Monitor Results and Learn from Experience

If supplier integration into new product development is to be a part of a company's long-term competitive strategy, regular evaluation and continuous improvement should be part of the process. One company includes evaluation as a formal step in its NPD process. Another company has developed a formal approach to disseminate lessons learned during supplier integration efforts throughout the company. After each development project is complete, a postaudit is conducted, and the project is examined for approaches that worked well or didn't work well. This information is shared throughout the organization via an intranet and is used to continuously improve the supplier integration process.

CONCLUSION

Three overall and important conclusions can be drawn from our work with companies that were integrating suppliers into NPD. First, supplier integration is growing in importance as a means to achieve competitive advantage. Companies that have successfully integrated suppliers into their new product development efforts have realized substantial improvements in cost, quality, and development time. Supplier integration into NPD will increase in the future and will occur at earlier stages of the NPD process.

Second, supplier integration should be guided by a strategic plan that is supported by the overall company structure and culture. Successful supplier integration requires a substantial management effort on the part of the buying company. Decisions to integrate suppliers must be made carefully to ensure that the potential benefits justify the effort. Furthermore, decisions to integrate suppliers must be made in the context of the firm's strategic business priorities and core competencies.

Finally, for companies that have decided to pursue a strategy of supplier integration, individual integration efforts must be managed carefully. A model execution process has been described that identifies key practices to facilitate successful supplier integration. Reengineering the new product development process and full deployment of supplier integration strategies and practices is not yet complete in most firms. The detailed findings from our research and benchmarking studies should provide actionable insights into how firms can maximize the benefits of supplier integration into new product development.

Chapter 3

Reengineering the New Product Development Process: Focus on Supplier Integration

"Change is inevitable—growth is optional."

Source unknown

INTRODUCTION

Radical reengineering changes to business processes and organizations are sweeping the globe, saving companies billions of dollars and rescuing companies and even nations from the brink of extinction—at least, according to many consultants and the popular press. However, after conducting in-depth case study interviews with 18 leading worldwide companies regarding their new product development (NPD) processes and their identification and utilization of supplier capabilities, we believe that many of the reengineering strategies and tactics these companies have used to become world class may not be considered radical at all. As a matter of fact, only one company interviewed discussed really radical changes to their process, although, as will be discussed, *radical* is a relative concept.

This is not to say that major changes were not made by the subject companies to support the NPD process. Indeed, various companies discussed changing their entire organizations from hierarchical, functionally focused vertical structures to flattened, horizontal, customer-focused organizations that emphasize teamwork. While such a change may require dedication of significant resources and be difficult to implement or downright painful in the short term (and, in some cases, the medium term), the business logic behind the move can no longer be considered radical. Although many large, medium, and small companies still may not have reorganized to fully leverage their most important asset (people) through cross-functional cooperation and flattened organizations, the strategy has been shown to make good business sense. It appears that the failure to drive organizational change and cross-functional cooperation to support NPD efforts is not hampered by the lack of recognition of the need for change, but rather by short-term performance concerns and resistance to change. With these preconditions in mind, there are perhaps three major and potentially radical changes in the NPD reengineering process: (1) establishing a long-term focus throughout the organization; (2) integrating non-company-affiliated suppliers into NPD efforts early and actively; and (3) implementing strategic and tactical changes systemwide.

The first potentially radical element of the NPD reengineering process is to establish a long-term focus within the organization. Subject companies indicated that reengineering the NPD process must begin with a long-term strategic vision of what the company's mission is and what businesses it will compete in and a clear definition of current and future core competencies. Only with this long-term perspective can the appropriate organizational structures, people, processes, and tools be developed to compete and survive in a rapidly changing global market.

A second potentially radical element of the NPD reengineering process, related to the first, is the integration of non-company-affiliated suppliers into the NPD process. Increasingly, companies that adopt and drive a long-term strategic orientation throughout their organization recognize that they neither need to be nor can they be the best at everything. They recognize the criticality of being the best at their core competencies and teaming with the best suppliers of noncore products and processes to develop the best possible value-added package. This change brings with it increasing importance for the procurement and supply chain organization to identify and develop world-class suppliers in support of NPD efforts.

The third and final potentially radical element of the NPD reengineering effort is to integrate all changes systemwide. Again, this process is directly tied to the long-term focus of the organization. Subject companies indicated that while they had effectively torn down the departmental walls in many cases, the tools and processes that were commonly used in one department were not effectively transferred and integrated throughout the organization. For example, one company indicated that it routinely provided the engineering group with extensive training in the CAD system, yet failed to leverage the full capabilities of this tool because it did not train other functional areas (for example, procurement) on how to potentially use the CAD data and system.

The lack of radical change discovered in the interviews does not indicate that companies have not realized substantial benefits from their reengineered NPD processes. Outcomes of a reengineered NPD process include significant hard benefits (such as reduced development costs, reduced NPD cycle time, improved quality, and reduced purchase price cost) as well as significant soft benefits (such as increased quality and frequency of communication, better decision making, identification of problems before they occur, and better coordination of NPD efforts). Thus, it is clear that both the significant and incremental changes made to support the NPD process, especially as they relate to integrating suppliers into NPD, have resulted in competitive and comparative advantage.

For the rest of this report, we will not be concerned with whether a change can be considered radical for two reasons. First, the companies interviewed indicated that no change would be ruled out unless it failed long-term cost-benefit analysis. Second, what is radical for one organization is old news for another. For example, one company had instituted cross-functional teamwork into its corporate culture in the 1970s, while others did not make this move until the late 1980s. Therefore, we will simply focus on the process of reengineering the NPD process to best leverage the capabilities and capacities of the organization, customers, and suppliers to best meet customer requirements.

REENGINEERING THE NPD PROCESS TO SUPPORT SUPPLIER INTEGRATION: AN OVERVIEW

The NPD reengineering process is driven by a series of interrelated questions at all levels of the organization as shown in Figure 3.1. Beginning with overall corporate strategy and driving through the business units' strategies as well as through functional level and key supplier strategies, each level in the value chain must ultimately ask itself: how are we helping meet customer requirements today, and how will we help meet anticipated customer requirements tomorrow? Only by asking—and of course answering—the questions shown in Figure 3.1 can the evolutionary and revolutionary changes necessary to remain ahead of the competition be identified and deployed.

The remainder of this section examines the changes that subject companies have made in their NPD process as a result of answering these questions. Table 3.1 and Table 3.2 identify the key strategic and execution NPD reengineering issues identified by subject

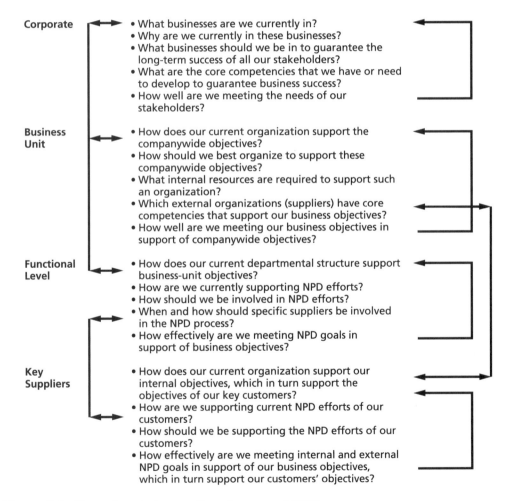

Figure 3.1. Key value chain questions to support NPD.

Table 3.1. Reengineering for NPD at the strategic level.

Key Strategic Issues

Nonintegrated NPD Strategy/Process	Integrated NPD Strategy/Process
NPD Strategy	**NPD Strategy**
• Lack of focused and integrated business and product strategies; internal design and development of all key components, subsystems, and systems without focused insourcing/outsourcing analysis and decision making	• Core business and core product strategies defined and well-communicated throughout the organization; focus on core technology development, allowing supplier integration into noncore yet critical systems based on detailed insourcing/outsourcing analysis
• Emphasis strictly on traditional purchasing skills in the procurement organization, such as supplier selection and negotiating skills	• Development of technical competence and strategic planning skills in the procurement organization
Organization Strategy	**Organizational Strategy**
• Hierarchical corporate organization, with formal lines of communication and limited empowerment of operational level employees	• Flattened corporate organization that facilitates free flow of information within and across operational units and provides decision-making responsibility, authority, and accountability throughout the organization
• No critical review/analysis of the current new product development process of continuous improvement opportunities	• Organizational culture that encourages and supports change not just for the sake of change, but for making improvements even when there is no apparent problem
• Functionally structured new product development efforts	• Product/service-focused and team-oriented new product development organization
Supply Chain Management Strategy	**Supply Chain Management Strategy**
• Limited long-term product and technology planning information-sharing with the supply base	• Alignment of key suppliers' long-term goals and objectives with the company's long-term goals and objectives through sharing of product and technical plans
• No strategic supplier alliances to develop new technologies or drive new product development	• Formation of strategic supplier alliances with joint identification of customer requirements and development of product concepts
• Limited or no support for supplier development; limited resource commitment from supplier for new product development	• Company dedicated resources to develop key suppliers' capabilities for integration into new product development; supplier investment in new capabilities and commitment of resources in the long term to new product development efforts

Table 3.2. Reengineering for NPD at the execution level.

Key Execution Issues	
Nonintegrated NPD Strategy/Process	**Integrated NPD Strategy/Process**
NPD Team Structure	**NPD Team Structure**

• Cross-functional team
  —Initial project team consisting strictly of engineering and R&D personnel
 	
  —Limited, superficial, or no cross-functional integration of procurement personnel
• Supplier integration
  —Little or no involvement of supplier(s)
  —Arbitrary selection of which supplier(s) to involve—often selected when problems occur
  —Suppliers of noncritical components often integrated
  —Integration limited to first-tier suppliers
	• Cross-functional team
	  —Cross-functional project team established from idea generation through production/operations volumes
	  —Procurement personnel members of the core team
	
	• Supplier integration
	  —Early involvement of supplier(s)
	  —Proactive selection and involvement of key supplier(s)—not just strategically aligned suppliers
	  —Only suppliers of critical components integrated
	  —First-tier, lower-tiered, and tooling suppliers may be integrated early

NPD Team Empowerment	**NPD Team Empowerment**
• Blind commitment to see new product development effort through to completion once the process has reached a certain point (e.g., dollars spent) • Key decision making under the strict control of upper management	• Stage gates at key points in the development process which yield a "go or no-go" decision by the cross-functional team, based on preestablished targets and criteria • Empowered project teams that can make key decisions, such as when a project should be delayed or even terminated
Supplier Selection	**Supplier Selection**
• Standard supplier qualification metrics (e.g., quality and cost) used in supplier selection process, with suppliers evaluated for integration concurrent with actual NPD efforts • Single functional area responsible for supplier selection	• Expanded set of new product development capability criteria (e.g., innovativeness, prototyping capabilities) used to preidentify/prequalify suppliers specifically for supplier integration efforts, prior to actual NPD opportunities • Cross-functional project team jointly assesses and selects the suppliers to be integrated

(continued)

Table 3.2.   Continued.

Key Execution Issues	
Nonintegrated NPD Strategy/Process	**Integrated NPD Strategy/Process**
NPD Roles and Responsibilities	**NPD Roles and Responsibilities**
• Project objectives —Buyer-driven performance specifications —Buyer-supplied business requirements —Lengthy bidding and negotiation process —Static performance requirements, with no motivation for long-term continuous improvement • Ownership —Buyer demands ownership rights to new product and process technologies	• Project objectives —Jointly developed performance specifications —Jointly developed business project targets (e.g., cost, time) —Target costing of supplied items —Inclusion in NPD agreement of continuous improvement objectives during production • Ownership —Agreement on ownership of jointly developed products and processes
Team Dynamics	**Team Dynamics**
• Colocation —Physically separated project teams —Arm's length relationship with supplier • Communication —Limited information-sharing with suppliers during new product development —Assign blame when problems arise, then expect the responsible party to resolve the issue	• Colocation —Internally colocated project team personnel —Supplier colocation as strategically appropriate, with fostering of team and partnering concepts • Communication —Open and direct function-to-function communication between buyer and supplier(s) —Joint identification and resolution of problems
Electronic Linkage	**Electronic Linkage**
• Limited use of linked information systems • Incompatible design tools	• Increased linking information systems, both internally and externally, to support communication • Increased use of aligned and linked design tools (e.g., CAD and parts databases) between buyer and supplier(s)

Table 3.2. Continued.

Key Execution Issues	
Nonintegrated NPD Strategy/Process	Integrated NPD Strategy/Process
Leveraging	**Leveraging**

• Standardization
  —Lack of building blocks between product generations with limited use of standard parts and processes
  —Designs developed without consideration of current capabilities
	• Standardization
	  —Increased use of modular designs, with increased use of standard parts and processes
	  —Designs that consider current and future internal and supplier process capabilities

• Supplier capabilities
  —Prototyping as the initial design nears completion
 	
  —All system final assembly performed in-house
	• Supplier capabilities
	  —Fast/early prototyping by and with suppliers prior to initial design completion
	  —Allowing for system level assembly in the supply chain

Risk Management	**Risk Management**
• No contingency planning • Contracts periodically reopened for competitive bidding • Single sourcing of product families	• Joint risk/reward agreements • Long-term contracts between the buyer and supplier for the life of the developed product • Single sourcing of a part number from the supplier responsible for the design; dual sourcing within the commodity family

companies, focusing on the role of suppliers and the procurement function in the process. Each of these issues is subsequently expanded on. The underlying message in this chapter is clear: reengineering the NPD process requires a long-term strategic focus beginning at the corporate level and driven throughout the entire organization as well as key supplier organizations.

SUPPLIER AND PROCUREMENT FUNCTION ROLES IN THE NPD PROCESS: KEY STRATEGIC ISSUES

The major strategic NPD reengineering issues identified in Table 3.1 are all interdependent strategies and processes. The strategic issues focus on long-term changes that are critical for enabling execution level processes. The strategic issues are grouped as: (1) NPD strategy; (2) organizational strategy; and (3) supply chain management strategy.

NPD Strategy

Know What You and Your Suppliers Are Good at.   A first major consideration in a company's NPD strategy is to identify and concentrate internal resources on core competencies and technologies. This strategic move is driven by multiple objectives, the most important of which is financial performance and ultimately stakeholder wealth. After years of extensive vertical integration all the way to the point of corporate-owned raw material supply, many companies have made and are continuing to make the move to vertically deintegrate. From a long-term business perspective, corporations have begun to realize that it is neither necessary nor profitable to do battle on their own. Rather, they focus on core competencies, such as marketing excellence, product innovation, or systems integration, and align suppliers with their business objectives in a linked value chain.

Nonintegrated	Integrated
• Lack of focused and integrated business and product strategies; internal design and development of all key components, subsystems, and systems without focused insourcing/outsourcing analysis and decision-making	• Core businesses and core product strategies defined and well-communicated throughout the organization; focus on core technology development, allowing supplier integration into noncore yet critical systems based on detailed insourcing/outsourcing analysis

CASE EXAMPLE

Focused Factory

One electronics company identified its NPD core competency as electronics design. The company maintains as much control of electronics design as possible. The company recognized that some suppliers have greater competencies in other areas, such as materials processing and product fabrication, and thus the company outsourced these activities. The company has also established a focus at each plant worldwide. The major domestic plants and over 100 plants worldwide have each been restructured as "focused factories." The company determined the key capabilities and capacities it needed to differentiate its products, and ensured that each plant developed and retained such capabilities. Some of the focused factories focus strictly on a single customer's needs. Other plants focus on either components for consumer products or OEM subassemblies. The goal is to grow the company through a focus on core competencies at each plant and to align suppliers in support of this objective.

CASE EXAMPLE

Broadcast Your Competency

Another electronics company has defined graphic display capabilities (for example, LCDs) as its core technology competency. The company communicated both internally and with key suppliers that graphics capabilities and quality are where it will differentiate its products from the competition. All displays, as well as some key semi-conductor requirements, are insourced. Essentially all other subsystems and components are now outsourced.

CASE EXAMPLE

Brilliant Discovery

This chemical company identified "discovery" as its core competency. Discovery in this case requires the combination of different raw materials and assessment of their effect on the environment in which they will be used. The company may screen thousands of new products during discovery before developing one that meets all requirements. The discovery-to-commercialization process may take five to seven years (which is considered fast for this industry), depending on environmental, health, and safety testing. The company indicated that it is in the best interests of its stakeholders to focus on discovery, and thus it no longer maintains the manufacturing capacity required to support the total manufacture of new, complex products. The company wants to get more products in the pipeline without adding people. By focusing on its core competency, the company has four times the number of new products in the pipeline, but the same number of employees as prior to execution of the focused strategy. Further, business volumes have doubled due to focus on the goal of discovery.

CASE EXAMPLE

Process Integration

Another manufacturing company indicates that it is the integration of over 800 process steps in the design of a new product where the company can most add value. Thus, major intermediate processes and final process design, which includes fabrication and assembly processes, form the core competency of the organization. Suppliers are not involved in overall process development, as their role is limited to their specific part of the process.

Hire and/or Develop the Right People. A second major consideration in a company's NPD strategy is to ensure that procurement personnel have the skills to support core competencies and new product development. As procurement personnel take on increasingly strategic roles in an organization, it is important for them to have the skills and resources necessary to make value-added contributions. For NPD efforts, this generally means that technical capabilities must be developed. Although it is not necessary for procurement personnel to be able to design new products, they must be able to understand and identify technology trends both internal and external to the company. This enables procurement to generate new product ideas, as well as evaluate the business and technical feasibility of ideas generated by others. Further, they must be able to develop a set of supplier selection criteria focused on technological capabilities as the role of suppliers in NPD continues to increase. These skills may be developed through internal or external training, job rotations, and active recruitment of engineering personnel into the procurement organization.

Nonintegrated	**Integrated**
• Emphasis strictly on traditional purchasing skills in the procurement organization, such as supplier selection and negotiating skills	• Development of technical competence and strategic planning skills in the procurement organization

CASE EXAMPLE

Back to School

At this electronics company, procurement personnel are primarily focused on commodity development and management, with involvement on NPD core teams limited to a secondary role. Still, procurement must support the NPD core teams as well as lead commodity development, making technical competence a must. Even before discussing specific applications, purchasing must: (1) identify and/or develop technologically capable suppliers; and (2) understand internal and external technology road maps to ensure alignment of key suppliers' goals and objectives with those of the firm. Technical training of current personnel and recruitment of technically competent employees have been used to meet these objectives. The company developed, in conjunction with a local university, a technical training class tailored for nontechnical staff, with company personnel providing the training. The company also influenced the management curriculum at the school to include an emphasis in some courses on technology and innovation management.

CASE EXAMPLE

Reinvent Purchasing

The purchasing organization at this consumer nondurable goods company has undergone significant change in recent years. Since 1960, the purchasing group was purely cost-focused with commodity purchasing of raw materials. The strategy was highly successful and survived basically unchanged until 1985, when the company began to realize that such a strategy would not yield the same benefits in a new environment characterized by greater domestic and global competition and increased negotiating position and strength of suppliers. The company's largest competitors recognized a need for change much earlier and by reconfiguring their purchasing organizations had been able to use supply chain management to competitive advantage. Thus, procurement's responsibilities were increased to include developing relationships both internal and external to the organization, ensuring linkage throughout the value-added chain, and providing internal functions with communication channels to suppliers. Procurement personnel were also assigned responsibility for assisting in the identification of new and innovative technology suppliers. Existing personnel were provided with technical training, and new recruits were assessed for their technical capabilities. The purchasing organization was thus restructured into a procurement and supply chain management organization, which now includes procurement, manufacturing, and logistics.

The company now relies on two types of sourcing specialists: material sourcing specialists and developmental sourcing specialists. The material sourcing specialist is responsible for purchasing materials to support the manufacture of existing products, with a focus on quality and cost. The developmental sourcing specialist is focused on identifying innovative new product and material ideas in the supply chain. The company believes it is critical to have a dedicated core of individuals assigned to developmental sourcing because if it assigns simultaneous responsibility for material and developmental sourcing, there will never be enough time for developmental sourcing.

Organizational Strategy

Subject companies identified three significant organizational changes to drive and support reengineering the NPD process. Although these high level organizational changes are driven by multiple strategic and business objectives, the focus of the following discussion is on how these changes relate to reengineering the NPD process.

Let People Make Decisions. One major organizational change is to switch from a highly formal hierarchical structure to a less formal and flatter organization. This change promotes cross-functional communication and cooperation and is structured to support a focus on core competencies. Companies have implemented such changes whether or not the motives were specific to reengineering the NPD process. That is, companies have realized that a flatter organization allows for greater effectiveness and higher efficiency in all functional areas regardless of whether the objective is NPD, accounting procedures, or total quality control.

Nonintegrated	Integrated
• Hierarchical corporate organization, with formal lines of communication and limited empowerment of operational level employees	• Flattened corporate organization that allows free flow of information in all operational units and provides decision-making responsibility, authority, and accountability throughout the organization

CASE EXAMPLE

Rebellion

This consumer nondurable goods company operates in five primary business sectors worldwide. At one time, the company was very centralized. All key marketing,

(continued)

manufacturing, and procurement decisions were made from corporate headquarters. The company underwent massive restructuring and change. In what was characterized as a "massive rebellion," the organization used a combination centralized/decentralized strategy to give greater authority/responsibility to local operating units. The company strategically centralized only the particular functions that could benefit from greater control and leverage, while leaving the remainder of the organization decentralized. Today, each of the five business sectors has complete profit-and-loss accountability. Decisions are made faster, employees are motivated, and profits are up across the board.

CASE EXAMPLE

Strategy Drives Structure

To become the world's leading company in its industry, this automotive company developed strategies to motivate employees and established the enablers to make the strategy work. Seven leadership strategies were identified:

1. Achieve worldwide growth (particularly through emerging markets)

2. Lead in customer satisfaction

3. Lead in corporate citizenship

4. Become the low-cost producer (value chain focus)

5. Achieve worldwide product excellence

6. Establish nimbleness through process leadership

7. Empower people

The company assessed its organizational structure prior to developing and implementing these strategies and realized that there was a low level of synergy and significant barriers to communication between functions. Three key conclusions from the organizational assessment are as follows:

- Operations were separated regionally, and even functionally within regions, which often led to conflicting objectives. During product development, for example, purchasing focused on costs after the start of production; product development focused on costs up to the start of production; manufacturing was often not even involved; while sales and marketing had to look for customers after the start of production.

- There was a low level of global process synergy. Unique regional vehicle platforms existed, for example. Also, a supplier supplying an identical part to operations in North America and Europe charged a significantly different price (beyond freight) to the two operations.

- Functions, particularly procurement, were reactive in all operational matters.

To implement the seven leadership strategies, the company realized that less formal communication and decision-making processes were required. Further, the company needed to make greater use of cross-functional teams and allow for greater responsibility and authority in those teams. Thus, the following organizational changes were made:

- A customer and product focus was established.
- Global decision-making processes were developed.
- Common product-based and cross-functional objectives were identified.
- Synergy across functions within regions and across regions was created.
- All appropriate functions were proactively involved in product design.
- Global product platforms with regional variants, as required for the market, were established.

Getting Accustomed to Change. Another significant organizational challenge is to create a culture that encourages and supports change and continuous improvement. Many companies have come to realize that a flexible company that is responsive to change is best able to meet customer requirements and is most likely to survive and thrive in the marketplace. Creating a corporate culture that is responsive to change may be the most challenging part of the whole NPD reengineering effort. In many companies, change is feared rather than viewed as an opportunity for growth. As a matter of fact, a global survey we conducted after the interviews were completed indicated that resistance to change was the most frequently cited barrier to reengineering the NPD process and integrating suppliers into NPD. The "not invented here" syndrome is, unfortunately, alive and well. The following case examples are drawn from the large-scale survey.

Nonintegrated	Integrated
• No critical review/analysis of the current new product development process for continuous improvement opportunities	• Organizational culture that encourages and supports change not just for the sake of change, but for making improvements even when there is no apparent problem

CASE EXAMPLE

Executive Leadership at the Buying Company Through Alignment

This consumer durable goods company indicated that its traditional corporate culture did not allow change in any aspect of operations, especially when it came to allowing external agents (suppliers) greater insight into the company's NPD plans. The key to overcoming this barrier was to conduct high-level meetings with appropriate executives

(continued)

to drive the alignment process prior to initiation of new projects. The short-term, intermediate-term, and long-term benefits of any change must be explicitly defined and quantified to drive acceptance of the proposed change.

CASE EXAMPLE

Executive Leadership at the Supplying Company Through Easy Wins

This computer company indicated that the corporate culture of one of its key suppliers lacked the flexibility to adapt to new and different methods of new product development. The solution was similar to the solution for overcoming internal barriers. The company conducted high-level meetings with the supplier presenting long-term, intermediate-term, and short-term benefits that were quantified to the greatest extent possible. The companies then selected initial supplier integration efforts that were low risk to demonstrate success and build momentum for change. As successes built, the companies formed a strategic alliance to ensure that short-, intermediate-, and long-term goals were aligned. Ongoing formal and informal communication helps ensure this alignment.

CASE EXAMPLE

"We Can Do It Better"

This engineering company indicated that resistance to change was not the fault of top management; instead functional departments drove the barrier, particularly engineering. The engineers felt that they were a very strong technical group and tended to discount those items that they did not develop. The belief persisted that if a product or process was not designed internally, the final product's quality and reliability would suffer. An initial step to overcoming this problem was to have engineering, program management, materials management, and senior management attend a concurrent product development seminar to educate them on the how-to and benefits of supplier integration. The company then formed a cross-functional team with technology groups to develop a process for integrating suppliers.

CASE EXAMPLE

"We Need to Make a Living"

This chemical company also faced resistance to change at the functional level rather than at the executive level. However, the resistance was driven by fear of losing jobs, skills, and controls rather than by fear of reduced product quality. To overcome this fear, the company clearly defined and communicated its core competencies to all personnel so that it was understood where supplier integration might and may not be used. Next, employees were educated about the added value of integration and assured that they will continue to work on core/added-value jobs. The company also used examples from industries that have used supplier integration successfully to motivate the change. Finally, the company instituted recognition programs that rewarded the use of supplier integration.

Platforms. Another significant organizational reengineering challenge, which is directly driven by the need to improve the NPD process, is to move from a functionally matrixed NPD organization to a product-focused or platform-matrixed team organization. This change is consistent with the overall organizational change to a flatter structure. For many years, the conventional wisdom indicated that a functional organization structure, characterized by personnel within any functional area (such as engineering or procurement) being matrixed to multiple projects or tasks, was the most efficient and effective use of resources. This was especially true as it related to NPD. Though new product teams were developed with some cross-functional support, the members of the team lacked an overall product focus. The team members may have supported multiple, nonrelated projects or product lines. For example, a manufacturing engineer may have supported the development of personal computers as well as mainframes. This makes it difficult to develop a sense of cradle-to-grave responsibility for any single product.

The trend indicated by our interviews is that companies are developing true cross-functional product-focused teams, with product responsibilities starting at concept development and continuing through production. A core team leads the process, with support teams and support personnel added as appropriate. Suppliers are also matrixed in, often with cradle-to-grave responsibilities for the product or product line they support.

Nonintegrated	Integrated
• Functionally structured new product development efforts	• Product/service-focused and team-oriented new product development organization

CASE EXAMPLE

Product-Focused Teams

An electronics company has begun to make this move toward true product teams. Though at a higher level each of its plants is focused on core products and product lines, the previous NPD structure did not support product-focused teams. For example, the company develops multiple electronic subassemblies in support of a single OEM product. In the old structure, it was not uncommon for a designer to be allocated to the design of multiple circuit board assemblies. These circuit boards may have been significantly different in terms of form, fit, and function and were integrated into a variety of higher-level assemblies. Under the new structure, a single system integration team leads the overall effort, which is supported by dedicated and focused subteams assigned responsibility for the development of a single circuit board assembly.

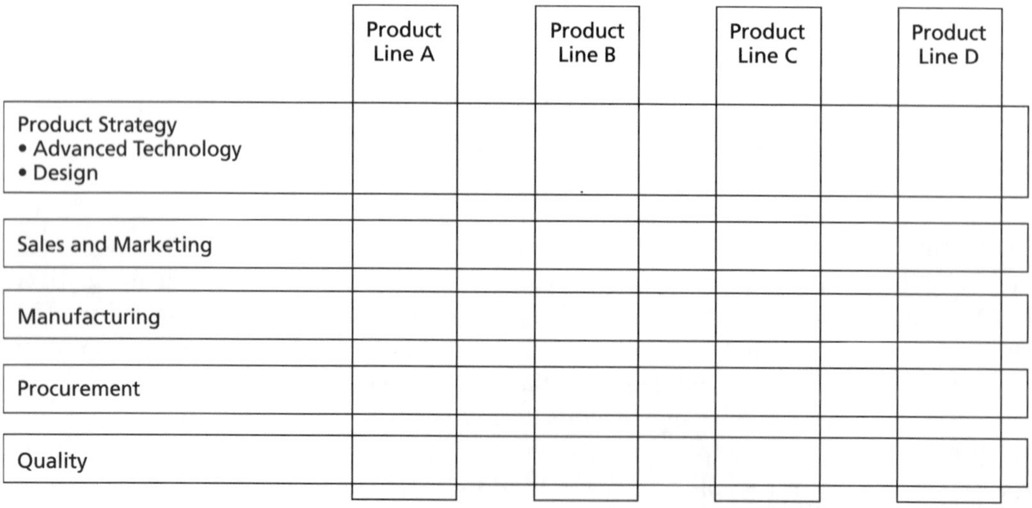

	Product Line A		Product Line B		Product Line C		Product Line D	
Product Strategy • Advanced Technology • Design								
Sales and Marketing								
Manufacturing								
Procurement								
Quality								

Figure 3.2. Matrixed NPD organization.

CASE EXAMPLE

Platform-Based NPD

An automotive company developed a product-focused team approach to NPD. The company moved to a product-based rather than input-based structure, as depicted in Figure 3.2. Operations were organized along primary product lines with a cross-functional focus to NPD. A core cross-functional team is assigned cradle-to-grave responsibility for the final product. Cross-functional subteams are also developed for major systems and subsystems within a specific product line, also with cradle-to-grave responsibility for that major input. Prior to the company's new strategy, the program manager was much like a customer to other departments. For example, engineers would work for supervisors on multiple projects. Now, there is basically a dedicated cross-functional staff within each vehicle that may be assigned to new product development efforts.

Supply Chain Management Strategy

Supply Chain Information Sharing. A major consideration in supply chain management strategy is to coordinate long-term business and technical strategies with those of the supply base in general and of critical suppliers in particular. This alignment of long-term goals and objectives is not limited to strategically allied suppliers. Rather, the objective is to ensure that the supply base as a whole understands where the company is headed so that suppliers are encouraged to align their internal operations and objectives with those of the buying company. This information sharing is also meant to encourage new entrepreneurial suppliers to seek out the company to propose new product ideas and to determine how they can develop the long-term capabilities and capacity to serve a large customer. Initially, the shared information may be very general. However, as familiarity and trust are developed, more detailed information is shared. In cases where time is critical, there may not be time to develop a strong trust, so nondisclosure and other legal agreements need to be implemented immediately. Alternatively, information sharing may occur with only well-known existing suppliers. Technology roadmaps and technology centers provide mechanisms for sharing long-term new product information.

Nonintegrated	Integrated
• Limited long-term product and technology planning information-sharing with the supply base	• Alignment of key suppliers' long-term goals and objectives with the company's long-term goals and objectives through sharing of product and technical plans

CASE EXAMPLE

"Blue Sky" Thinking

One electronics company established advanced technology centers to share long-term information and align buyer-supplier objectives. Long-range planning with a horizon 5 to 10 years out drives "blue sky" thinking, as supplier involvement focuses on technology development and not specific product requirements, although the intention of discussing any technology is to either create or support specific product requirements in the future. It is especially critical during this long-term planning for the commodity teams and procurement personnel in particular to access, understand, and influence internal and supplier technology road maps. Both companies will present their road maps, and the company tries to match its needs with the supplier. The company may even change its needs based on the supplier's presentation. The company's technology maps contain performance curves with expected targets by date. Each curve has a "sweet spot," which suppliers are encouraged to target. If a supplier cannot be at the sweet spot by the target date, they will not get the business. The advanced technology center provides the first opportunity to narrow potential suppliers for future product lines. This company notes that in many cases a supplier may be a direct competitor or supply a direct competitor. Thus, the company is cautious about how much information it shares and makes extensive use of nondisclosure agreements in such cases.

CASE EXAMPLE

Window of Technology

This automotive company's new strategy established a "window of technology" process that provides a neutral corner for suppliers to share their technology road maps with a single point of contact at the company without fear of having internal company departments hearing (stealing) their ideas. This process occurs under the direction of advanced technology teams. Existing or new suppliers are welcome to present their

(continued)

ideas. Promising yet unproven ideas can be further investigated in the company's scientific research lab. The window of technology resolves problems of suppliers not knowing how to approach the company with new product ideas. It also ensures that suppliers will get a firm answer if the company is interested in their products. The company has emphasized to suppliers that it does not plan to develop a technology for the bookshelf unless it has useful market implications. In the past, suppliers might develop technologies that never made it to market. Now, the company is giving suppliers more detailed and longer range market information and forecasts. The supply base has been very receptive to this process.

Technology Chats

At this electronics company, the long-term information-sharing process depends on whether the goal is basic research or new product planning. During basic research, the process tends to be more formal and controlled. Specific suppliers are approached and asked if they are willing to work on technology development for a potential new product. Information-sharing takes place during joint meetings with suppliers, beginning with top management, to gain mutual commitment. Although the process is formal, there are no formal contracts, as the key to success is building and maintaining trust. However, the trend is toward increased use of confidentiality agreements, as the company has to disclose more detailed and proprietary information about the entire product line in order to drive innovation in the supply base. For these basic technologies, R&D leads discussions, with procurement sitting in but not taking an active role.

During the new product planning stage, the process is less formal. The company provides multiple suppliers with performance requirements and some preliminary specifications at least three generations ahead of when the new products are planned for introduction. Suppliers are also provided with estimated time frames for volume shipment and long-term volume projections. In some cases, suppliers are also informed of target costs. This long-term information-sharing allows the company's suppliers to develop the capability and capacity to meet future needs. The engineering group and to some extent procurement are primarily involved at this stage and may provide suppliers with engineering mock-ups or breadboards to stimulate innovation.

Technology Road Maps

This computer company shares technology road maps with only critical suppliers (such as CPU suppliers) to ensure that the company's technology needs are known to suppliers and are in line with the suppliers' plans. The company looks at least two product generations ahead with the road maps. The company's road maps, as well as the supplier's road maps, may be altered after the information is shared. The company tries to get features that are needed for future products designed into industry-leading suppliers' standard chip sets. The company's road maps specify plans related to (1) LCD size and resolution; (2) required CPU speed and features; (3) main memory size; (4) hard disk size and capacity; and (5) pricing.

CASE EXAMPLE

Product, Process, and Automation Road Maps

This electronics and aerospace company develops road maps that project technology and new product applications five years out. From the product road map, the company constructs process-technology road maps and automation road maps three years out. Moreover, expected growth patterns and needs in the company's markets of interest are identified. These road maps are discussed with key suppliers. Further, suppliers are expected to present similar road maps to ensure alignment.

CASE EXAMPLE

Putting the Ball in the Supplier's Court

This company indicates that it encourages suppliers to make technology presentations to the R&D and engineering staff to create and nurture new product ideas. Suppliers may also be brought to the company's plants to help identify how the suppliers' materials and products might be applicable to potential new products. The process is informal, and it is largely the responsibility of suppliers to take the initiative to share long-term information.

Supply Chain Relationships. Another significant change in supply chain management strategy, closely related to long-term information-sharing change, is to form strategic partnerships with suppliers for technology and new product development. These alliances are established so that each company views each new venture as a shared business opportunity and risk. That is, each company makes a commitment to new ventures well before there is clear evidence that a new product will ever reach the design stage, much less the actual production stage. The companies work together to understand and define the final customers' requirements. They jointly commit time, money, capital, and personnel to generating new product concepts and ideas. They complement each other's core competencies by developing an intimate understanding of each other's operations and business plans. These relationships develop over time, as each company learns more about the other through successes and, perhaps even more importantly, failures.

Nonintegrated	**Integrated**
• No strategic supplier alliances to develop new technologies or drive new product development	• Formation of strategic supplier alliances with joint identification of customer requirements and development of product concepts

CASE EXAMPLE

Choose Fewer Dance Partners

This electronics company attempts to minimize the number of allied suppliers because it is concerned about becoming too dependent on any single supplier. The company has put a significant amount of effort into standardizing its parts and processes as well using modular designs to help minimize the need for supplier partnerships. The company's general philosophy is to select whoever is the best at the time. However, the company has formed partnerships with a handful of suppliers who have consistently proven to be technology leaders. These partnerships are focused much more on technology development than new products per se. In cases in which joint technology development is the goal, the company believes there is a much greater need for supplier partnerships because both companies make a significant resource commitment. The company will conduct partnership meetings at least once a year with its few supplier partners to ensure alignment and build trust. Note that although the company performs trust-building exercises, it repeatedly stated that performance over time was the best mechanism for trust and partnership development.

CASE EXAMPLE

Engineering and Sourcing Matrices

This chemical company indicates that it has a total supply base of approximately 200 capable suppliers. Though not considered supplier alliances or partnerships, some suppliers clearly have closer relationships with the company than others. These close suppliers have consistently provided innovative and high-quality inputs toward final product development and receive a "preferred supplier" status. For example, if a process involves 30 suppliers, maybe 8 to 12 of those will have a close relationship with the company. Further, the close suppliers will receive 80 percent of the purchase dollars for the new product. The remaining suppliers provide commonly produced items. The company believes there are very few opportunities for alliances, yet still wants closer, more integrative relationships with key suppliers. The company developed an engineering matrix to categorize the nature of equipment and the work processes needed to secure inputs and a sourcing matrix to identify the type of relationship that should be developed with any supplier. These matrices are shown in Figure 3.3 and Figure 3.4 respectively.

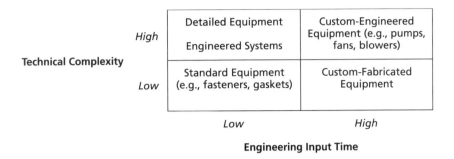

Figure 3.3. Engineering matrix.

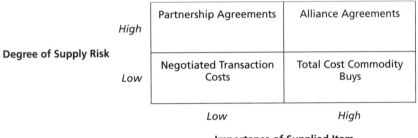

Figure 3.4. Sourcing matrix.

Not All Suppliers Are Equal

This aerospace company indicates that there are three types of suppliers: alliances, partners, and traditional. In all cases, only supplier alliances are included in NPD. There are currently 15 alliances within this company, one in each of the strategic commodity areas. Strategic alliance suppliers willingly invest in changing their fundamental business practices to reduce duplication and waste and facilitate improved performance. Firms have joint ownership in the relationship and equally share in the benefits and risks of managing the relationship.

Supply Chain Development. Another major change in supply chain management strategy is to invest in the capabilities of critical suppliers, both allied and nonpartner suppliers, with the expectation or requirement that suppliers will make reciprocal investments and commitments to support new technology and new product development. Supplier development strategies to support new product development are increasingly implemented by leading companies to ensure that the supply base is capable of meeting short-, intermediate-, and long-term needs. The objective of supplier development depends on the needs. For example, a supplier known for developing innovative new products may lack a total quality focus in production so that there are production yield problems. The buying company may provide TQM training or help analyze the supplier's processes to resolve the problem. The key is to allocate the company's potentially limited resources to developing only those suppliers critical to the long-term health of the firm.

Nonintegrated	Integrated
• Limited or no support for supplier development; limited resource commitment from suppliers for new product development	• Company dedicated resources to develop key suppliers' capabilities for integration into new product development; supplier investment in new capabilities and commitment of resources in the long-term to new product development efforts

CASE EXAMPLE

Focus on Key Technology Suppliers

This electronics company only recently adopted a supplier development strategy. In many cases, the company believes that market forces are enough to ensure a capable supply base. However, over time the company has identified critical technology suppliers that may need improvement in certain areas, such as quality or cost reduction. In such cases, the commodity management teams take on the responsibility. The company has moved from a reactive mode of fixing problems as they occur to a proactive mode of preventing problems. A high level of resources may be committed to development efforts, with the formal understanding that continuous improvement and cost reductions are expected in return. The company also provides feedback and in some cases resources to suppliers not selected for NPD efforts to motivate suppliers to develop next generation technologies and products.

CASE EXAMPLE

Risk-Sharing

This computer company begins talking with suppliers as the discovery process comes to a close, which is about one to one-and-a-half years into a five-to-seven-year concept-to-customer development cycle. The company indicates that close or preferred suppliers must be willing to spend development money early, with no guarantee that the product will ever be produced commercially. The company provides suppliers with technical support for the modification or retrofit of existing equipment to minimize capital expenses that may not provide required financial returns. Suppliers do not necessarily start working five years prior to launch, but they know they must be ready. For a full supply of compounds or raw materials, suppliers need one to two years' warning. This is the point when most major supplier investments occur.

It Helps to Be a Good Customer

This electronics company indicates that finding capable suppliers is generally not a problem, as suppliers seek the company out, not the other way around. One of the biggest challenges is finding ways to turn down suppliers without getting sued! However, the pool of equipment suppliers is relatively small (600 to 800 worldwide in five regions). In some cases, there may only be one small supplier producing a given piece of equipment. In such cases, the company will commit resources and financial support to develop the supplier's capability and capacity. In cases where no existing equipment will satisfy the company's needs, it will work with the most capable supplier of that equipment in a joint development effort.

SUPPLIER AND PROCUREMENT FUNCTION ROLES IN THE NPD PROCESS: KEY EXECUTION ISSUES

Assuming that the necessary strategies and organizational structure are in place to support supplier integration into NPD, a company can successfully address the critical execution issues. Key execution issues related to the reengineering of the NPD process include changes to: (1) NPD team structure, (2) NPD team empowerment, (3) supplier selection, (4) NPD roles and responsibility, (5) team dynamics, (6) electronic linkage, (7) leveraging, and (8) risk management. There is a high degree of interdependence among many of these major categories of changes, as well as among the specific changes within each major group.

NPD Team Structure

Cross-Functional and Procurement Involvement. A major change to the NPD team structure is early cross-functional involvement, with increased procurement involvement. Many potential benefits may be realized from early cross-functional involvement. Perhaps most importantly, it brings a wide variety of perspectives and skills into the design process so that critical issues and problems are addressed early. Since the design process locks up the majority of the total cost of a product and the cost of solving problems increases exponentially after a design release, it makes sense to bring as much knowledge and as many resources as possible into the process early. Cross-functional involvement may also build long-term commitment and ownership of the project throughout the organization. Procurement personnel may make significant contributions through early involvement by identifying new technologies and the most appropriate suppliers for the project, for example.

Nonintegrated	**Integrated**
• Cross-Functional Team	• Cross-Functional Team
—Initial project team consisting strictly of engineering and R&D personnel	—Cross-functional project team established from idea generation through production/operations volumes
—Limited, superficial, or no cross-functional integration of procurement personnel	—Procurement personnel members of the core team

CASE EXAMPLE

Ongoing Activity

This automotive company has formalized its supplier integration into NPD strategy. The strategy indicates that procurement's involvement in NPD is not a "point in time" activity. Rather, procurement is involved both strategically and tactically throughout the NPD effort. Procurement personnel, through membership on advanced technology and commodity management teams, are responsible for overall supply-base strategy. Major strategic objectives include the following:

1. Develop a global supply base

2. Identify and assess new technologies

3. Drive for design and technology commonality both within and across business units

4. Leverage worldwide volumes

5. Drive continuous improvement

Procurement personnel on the specific product teams are responsible for tactical purchasing processes that include the following:

1. Implementing the strategic work plan

2. Selecting suppliers from the recommended supply base

3. Performing the actual purchasing function

4. Assessing supplier performance and providing feedback to strategic purchasing

CASE EXAMPLE

Core NPD Team

One electronics company made a significant shift to NPD core teams in 1993. The structure includes a core team, extended teams, and support members. The core teams typically consist of six people: the team leader, a mechanical engineer, an electrical engineer, a manufacturing engineer, a software engineer, and, depending on the application, a representative from another department, such as operations or quality. Procurement generally does not have a formal member on the core team. The company believes that the procurement department's role does not warrant full-time participation, since procurement resources are limited relative to the number of NPD teams. However, procurement does play a major role on support and subteams. Suppliers may be members of the core team.

Although the company's reengineering effort called for allocating 100 percent of each team member's time to the core team, resource constraints made this model impossible. However, to the extent possible, personnel are assigned to core teams that address similar product and project objectives. The key is to ensure that the team leader remains on the project from concept to production. Further, it is more important to have systems in place, than to have people in place to ensure continuity. That is, people may change, but the roles and capabilities in each position should not. This company also indicates that a cross-functional team reviews project status at each stage in the new product development effort and makes the appropriate "go or no-go" decision. The design is compared to preestablished performance, cost, and time-to-volume targets. Of course, simply failing to meet objectives is not enough to cancel a project. The team must identify exactly why the project should be terminated (for example, the technology is not currently commercially feasible but may be at a particular date in the future).

CASE EXAMPLE

Changing Team Composition

This electronics company indicated that laboratory work is an important first step in any NPD process. The research and development lab is responsible for developing technologies that are put on the bookshelf. These technologies may be developed internally or jointly with suppliers and are considered for new product projects when they are technically and commercially feasible. Cross-functional teams are involved throughout, although the composition of the team depends on the stage of development. A project team is formed before new product planning and consists initially of design, manufacturing, and marketing personnel. Procurement is typically not directly involved until the prototype design phase, which occurs early in the NPD effort. This company also monitors new product and supplier performance throughout the development process. With new suppliers, a full audit may be undertaken during the prototype design phase. Performance is measured relative to preestablished cost, quality, performance, and schedule targets.

CASE EXAMPLE

Proving Procurement's Added Value

This company indicated that internal research and development and engineering have begun working with procurement on new material and new product development efforts, but that the relationship is not yet well-developed. Some engineers have been resistant to such changes, which they perceive as reducing or undermining their authority in NPD. As a result, procurement has slowly transitioned into NPD teams by presenting engineers with available data about materials, costs, and supplier capabilities, and letting engineers make the decision whether to integrate certain suppliers. Procurement recognizes that in many cases, research and development may already know who the best suppliers are, based on past experience. However, research and development may not have the time to identify new suppliers. Through this process, procurement will develop a stronger, more trusting relationship with their engineering counterparts, which is essential for the product-supply concept and greater cross-functional involvement in NPD. This reflects a significant change at the company, with managers of all departments clearly on line with this philosophy.

Supplier Involvement. Another major change to the NPD team structure is the strategic integration of suppliers, potentially from different levels within the value-chain, into new product development efforts. This change calls for key suppliers to be actively involved in the decision-making process for the product or service they are providing and potentially for the final product or service in which their input will be used. There should be no predefined limit on the type or number of suppliers involved. Rather, each supplier and each input should be evaluated for the importance of its contribution to the team effort and be involved at the appropriate level. This may mean involvement on the core or final product team or on lower-level support teams. The evaluation also minimizes the number of suppliers involved, keeping team size manageable. As with cross-functional teaming, the objective is to bring the suppliers' expertise into the design process as early as possible to maximize value added and minimize future engineering changes.

Nonintegrated	Integrated
• Supplier Integration —Little or no involvement of supplier(s)	• Supplier Integration —Early involvement of supplier(s)
—Arbitrary selection of which supplier(s) to involve—often selected when problems occur	—Proactive selection and involvement of key supplier(s)—not just strategically aligned suppliers
—Suppliers of noncritical components often integrated	—Only suppliers of critical components integrated
—Integration limited to first-tier suppliers	—First-tier, lower-tiered, and tooling suppliers may be integrated early

CASE EXAMPLE

Component Driven Strategy

This electronics company indicated that an initial key step in the NPD process is to identify those items that will benefit from supplier integration. During the NPD planning stage, the internal cross-functional team identifies key components that are candidates for outsourcing. Key components are those

1. That have long procurement lead times

2. That internal designers and engineers are uncertain of exact specifications appropriate to meet performance requirements

3. Whose performance is critical to the performance of the finished product to achieve customer satisfaction

4. That require unique processing or materials

5. That have high manufacturing cost

6. Whose anticipated production volumes exceed internal manufacturing capacity or capability

Large-scale integrated circuit suppliers are integrated earliest into the process because they have the longest ramp-up time (5 to 6 months) and other technologies are dependent on a frozen design.

CASE EXAMPLE

Early Integration of Critical Suppliers

Another electronics company indicated that initial market research to generate new product ideas and first product planning are performed by internal teams. The earliest point at which suppliers are integrated is during the technology research phase of NPD, during which technology alternatives are evaluated. At this stage, mainly integrated circuit suppliers are involved, as ICs are the most critical components (other than internally supplied display units) and because ICs have the longest development time. Suppliers of other components such as keyboards, disk drives, and mechanical parts may be integrated in later stages, such as component or final product planning.

CASE EXAMPLE

Joint Development and Licensing

This chemical company indicated that suppliers will not generally be actively involved during the product discovery phase, which this company has identified as a core

(continued)

competency. An exception occurs when another company has developed a new molecule, but lacks either the capability to perform full application and environmental design verification testing or the capability to determine how the molecule can be made commercially feasible. In such cases, joint development may be pursued, with patent rights negotiated. The company may also license molecules from a university, for example, to determine commercial applications. Once discovery nears completion and patent rights are filed, suppliers may be integrated into the new product commercialization phase. High-impact suppliers who identify new technology applications and process techniques for new molecules may be integrated as discovery nears completion. These high-impact suppliers may be given a single sheet discussion of the final molecule and be instructed to figure out how to make the intermediary. Other key suppliers may then become involved where the detailed application design, start-up, and implementation begin.

<hr>

CASE EXAMPLE

Staged Integration Process

This electronics company uses a staged process for supplier integration into new process development. Early in the life of a process or a factory, when equipment and processes are under development, the need for supplier-provided services and the potential ROI from the supplier's involvement is large. For example, supplier expertise is needed to develop preventive maintenance routines, troubleshooting guidelines, and so on. Internal technicians cannot typically be used in the early stages of production, since they are not as well-trained and the level of service required exceeds capacity levels. Later in the life of the factory, supplier-provided service begins to have a negative ROI. A fully trained internal technician will be as capable as a supplier technician but will cost a lot less, perhaps $20,000 to $60,000 less per year. Further, internal technicians may be cross-trained to further reduce head count when different peak production loads occur. As production increases, there is a transition from external technicians to internal technicians, as supplier technician responsibility changes from repair and maintenance to on-the-job training of internal technicians.

<hr>

CASE EXAMPLE

Focus on Core Competencies

This consumer nondurable goods company has not traditionally integrated suppliers in early stages of NPD. However, the company plans to bring suppliers into the idea generation phase of NPD in the future. The company recognizes that it must make every effort to simplify the process. Involving suppliers in idea generation permits the company to transition greater responsibility to suppliers and thus simplify internal processes by focusing on core competencies. The company is attempting to emphasize the communication of performance specifications instead of physical property specifications to suppliers and allow the suppliers room to innovate. The company has also informed first-tier suppliers that they are now responsible for integrating their own lower-tier suppliers' technologies and skills.

NPD Team Empowerment

A major change to NPD decision making is the empowerment of cross-functional teams to make critical technical and business decisions. The main objective of this change is to drive ownership of the NPD process through the organization by assigning responsibility and authority to the appropriate level. This does not imply assigning complete authority to project teams for all decisions; rather it calls for clearly identifying what decisions the team can make without review (for example, supplier selection), which decisions require management review and approval (for example, major investment in new equipment, or termination of a project), and which decisions are the sole responsibility of upper management (for example, financing the project).

Nonintegrated	Integrated
• Blind commitment to see new product development effort through to completion once the process has reached a certain point (e.g., dollars spent)	• Stage gates at key points in the development process which yield a "go or no-go" decision by the cross-functional team, based on preestablished targets and criteria
• Key decision making under the strict control of upper management	• Empowered project teams that can make key decisions, such as when a project should be delayed or even terminated

CASE EXAMPLE

Terminate Power

This electronics company indicates that it has occasionally had to terminate a relationship with a supplier involved in design work when it became apparent the supplier would be unable to deliver on preestablished targets. The company will work with the supplier to develop the necessary capabilities before terminating the relationship. The decision to terminate belongs to the project team, although procurement is ultimately responsible for the decision. In one case, a projected volume shipment date indicated that a project would be delayed so much that it would already be technologically outdated at the time of market entry. The product was therefore canceled at the design for volume stage, even though it had already gone through design verification.

Just Do It

This electronics company indicates that it simply cannot allow a single process out of 800 integrated processes to cause the termination of a new product development effort. Problems in process design are typically not discovered until initial process integration. For example, the company may find out that a supplier has committed to specifications that the equipment is not capable of meeting, especially when the equipment has never been built before. The deficiency may be innocent, or the supplier may have just been trying to get the company's business. Either way, with a huge investment made in the other processes, the project team cannot terminate the project because all processes are so closely integrated that pulling equipment off the floor will create problems throughout the facility. The team must therefore live with a deficiency or work with the supplier or other suppliers to bring the equipment up to requirements. If a design change is required, the costs of the change must be negotiated, although the supplier is generally held liable.

Product-Planning Manual

This automotive company developed a new product-planning manual that details the tasks that must be accomplished at each stage of a NPD effort, indicates who has responsibility for that task, and names the major deliverables for each task. A simplified version of the product-planning process model is shown in Figure 3.5.

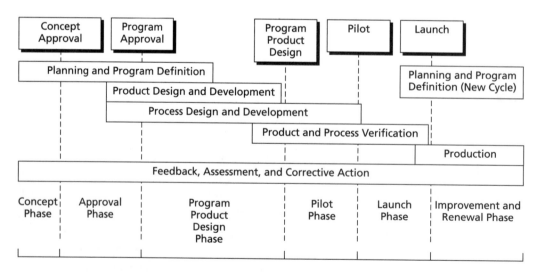

Figure 3.5. Product planning process model.

Major milestones or stage gates are incorporated into each phase to ensure that all requirements are met before proceeding. For example, concept approval must be received prior to final program approval and before actual product/process design and development can begin. Within each phase, there are major milestones or gates that are more directly under the control of the NPD team. These milestones identify the major deliverables, key measures, and tools and processes the NPD team may use to make a decision at that point. For example, during the pilot phase, a key milestone is to freeze the plant process. Responsibility for this task is assigned to the systems and/or component level product assurance teams, with lead actions assigned to manufacturing and suppliers as appropriate. The objective is to solidify the plant process so that setup and verification can begin. Subtasks include reviewing the plant layout, process flowcharts, and preventive maintenance plans. Deliverables include a refined plant layout, process flowcharts, and preventive maintenance plans. Methods and tools suggested to complete these tasks include design of experiments and process failure mode and effects analysis. Two measures the team must use to make a decision to proceed are the number of process operation description sheets available divided by the number required, and the number of key process characteristics for which established quality goals are in jeopardy of being reached divided by the total number of key process characteristics. The planning manual also lists periodic review questions the team should address regardless of whether a major milestone is soon approaching. Key questions include: "Have component packaging standards and shipping plans been documented and how will they be tested?" "Have process sign-offs been conducted at your supplier locations yet?" "What is the status of gauge calibration and test equipment plans?"

Supplier Selection

A major change to supplier assessment and selection for integration into NPD is the use of cross-functional teams to develop project specific criteria and to ultimately make the final supplier selection decision. Many companies that started to integrate suppliers found that their supplier evaluation criteria lacked the measures required to support supplier selection for integration into NPD. Traditional criteria may have covered cost and quality, but they lacked evaluation of long-term technical performance, responsiveness to changing requirements, and ability to work on teams, for example. Further, supplier selection was often the sole responsibility of procurement, which often emphasized cost at the expense of other parameters, or engineering, which often emphasized technology at the expense of other issues and brought the supplier in through the back door. Making the selection through a team process, even if one function takes the lead role, assures that all parameters are addressed and prioritized.

Nonintegrated	Integrated
• Standard supplier qualification metrics (e.g., quality and cost) used in supplier selection process, with suppliers evaluated for integration concurrent with actual NPD efforts	• Expanded set of new product development capability criteria (e.g., innovativeness, prototyping capabilities) used to preidentify/prequalify suppliers specifically for supplier integration efforts, prior to actual NPD opportunities
• Single functional area responsible for supplier selection	• Cross-functional project team jointly assesses and selects the suppliers to be integrated

CASE EXAMPLE

Purchasing's Veto Power

This electronics company recently began using NPD core teams. Procurement is not generally part of the core team because of resource constraints, but supplier selection decisions are made through a consensus between the core team and procurement. However, because procurement drives supplier development and manages the supplier relationships, they retain veto power in the supplier selection process. The company uses commodity management teams of three to seven core members to assess and approve suppliers in each commodity area and develop a list of approved suppliers. One concern this created was that suppliers not on a preapproved list would no longer develop and innovate for the company. This concern was alleviated by including engineering on supplier assessment teams and by allowing new or existing suppliers not on the list to discuss new technologies and product ideas in a confidential setting. The company indicates that traditional cost, quality, and delivery criteria will always be critical, but that such measures are simply order qualifiers. The company now also emphasizes interim performance measures, such as meeting milestones, as well as cycle-time reduction and team performance.

CASE EXAMPLE

Situation-Based Team Leadership

This electronics company evaluates all suppliers using a formal certification process. Standard metrics include quality, cost, and delivery. However, supplier selection for integration into NPD is based on a supplier's capability to design and manufacture a product in large volume within the required time. Length of the relationship and prior experience are two major considerations in the selection decision. Very rarely is a new supplier integrated into NPD or chosen to provide key components or subassemblies. This company indicates that engineering generally takes the lead in selecting a supplier when new technology is being developed, while procurement takes the lead once the actual NPD process begins. In both cases, procurement has final authority, but it is rare that engineering's selection of a new technology developer is vetoed. This issue is generally not a problem, since procurement and engineering work together as a team throughout NPD and because the selection process is limited by the structure of the industry and the relatively small number of available suppliers.

CASE EXAMPLE

Site Visits

At this computer company, design, manufacturing, and procurement personnel conduct site visits to evaluate potential suppliers for integration into NPD. Although cost and quality remain key criteria, the company indicates that it now assesses the supplier's long-term technical capabilities as well. This long-term focus has become critical because technology is changing very rapidly, and the company believes it can keep costs down in the long run by early identification of innovative suppliers. Engineering and procurement jointly select suppliers, with engineering playing the stronger role in the decision when innovation is critical. Engineering performs a technical evaluation of potential suppliers, while procurement handles contract negotiations.

CASE EXAMPLE

Prequalified Suppliers

This electronics company maintains a list of approximately 180 process and equipment suppliers prequalified for integration into new process development. To make the list, a supplier must undergo extensive commercial and technical evaluation and an exhaustive selection process. Once a supplier is designed into a process, it generally remains there for five to seven years because there are significant switching costs to change suppliers. For example, the cost to install a new piece of equipment exceeds $200,000. Further, disruptions to the manufacturing process are extremely expensive. In selecting equipment suppliers, the cross-functional team performs a risk assessment that includes a detailed ROI estimate. This is typically based on a few test lots produced in a lab, which may or may not reflect what actually occurs on the shop floor where there is a dedicated crew producing large volumes. Based on the lab results, the supplier's performance history is considered and a conservative estimate of the supplier's actual capability is made.

Cross-Division Coordination

This automotive company prequalifies suppliers based on quality, cost, and delivery. Extra criteria are used and weighted to select suppliers for supplier integration. Different members of the cross-functional NPD team will lead the process depending on project needs (for example, engineering performs engineering capability analysis). Previous experience in NPD integration is a plus when evaluating suppliers. Although the company prefers to use suppliers within its current supply base, it does not hesitate to use new suppliers if existing suppliers cannot meet current needs. The project team also accesses a companywide database that identifies suppliers used across multiple divisions to aid the selection process. The final decision to integrate a supplier is ultimately the responsibility of the general manger of the strategic business unit, who reviews the recommendation of the cross-functional team.

NPD Roles and Responsibilities

Joint Buyer/Supplier Planning. A significant change in supplier integration efforts is to jointly define business and technical requirements for the NPD effort. This includes not only design requirements, but project and business objectives such as cost and schedule as well. Further, jointly defined goals should extend beyond the design and development effort to include ongoing production objectives for the new product. Each party brings its expertise to the table so that realistic yet aggressive project goals can be set.

Nonintegrated	Integrated
• Project objectives	• Project objectives
—Buyer-driven performance specifications	—Jointly developed performance specifications
—Buyer-supplied business requirements	—Jointly developed business project targets (e.g., cost, time)
—Lengthy bidding and negotiation process	—Target costing of supplied items
—Static performance requirements, with no motivation for long-term continuous improvement	—Inclusion in the NPD agreement of continuous improvement objectives during production

Developing Cost Targeting Skills

This electronics company increasingly wants to use cost targets to drive the design and development of supplied items. However, there is a general concern that the company currently lacks the skills required to develop cost targets for components and subsystems. The challenge is especially difficult in high-tech areas where suppliers may have significant differences in their processes and the technical nature of their materials. Thus, the company feels a need to use the bidding process for market lever-age to ensure a fair price, though the goal is to move toward target costing. On some projects, the company may solicit many quotes to get a feel for the market before starting to develop target costs. In cases where a supplier partner is being used, the company does not solicit bids. Rather, the company works up front with the partner, as opposed to initially developing a target internally. To some extent, the company will continue to use the bid process to at least imply market competition, but the com-pany is currently providing the procurement group with training in Value Analysis/Value Engineering, Activity-Based Costing, and Total Cost Analysis. This company continually encourages suppliers to improve and has formalized a supplier continu-ous improvement strategy that becomes part of any NPD effort. Approximately 16 percent of the supplier's quarterly rating involves whether the supplier provides improvement ideas. Suppliers are encouraged to submit improvement ideas that are first reviewed and logged by procurement, then sent to the appropriate engineering group. After VA/VE with a cross-functional team that includes the supplier, a deci-sion to accept or reject the idea is made. This VA/VE process is publicized and stressed during meetings with suppliers.

CASE EXAMPLE

Requirements Package

At this electronics company, all new products are designed to target costs. Target cost is first established for the final product through internal analysis of markets, and then cost targets are established for each component group in the product. The initial breakdown is again based on the company's internal engineering expertise and prior experience with similar products. Although suppliers are not directly involved in establishing cost targets, the targets are negotiable to some extent. Cost targets, as well as quality and performance targets, are part of the basic require-ments package delivered to potential suppliers. If the potential supplier can identify why a target should be moved (for example, marginal product performance improvement greatly exceeds cost increase), the company will consider new targets.

CASE EXAMPLE

Life-Cycle Targets

This company indicates that it includes cost saving requirements over the long term in all NPD agreements with suppliers. There is no sharing of cost savings—the company benefits from any and all cost savings the supplier comes up with. Consequently, there

(continued)

appears to be little incentive for the supplier to come up with cost saving ideas. However, there is an unwritten understanding between the companies that suppliers who develop cost saving processes can expect future increased volumes and preferred supplier status.

Target Management

At this automotive company, strategic planning teams set minimal acceptable worldwide customer requirements limits in a number of areas (such as weight, quality, and cost). The development team then writes a development specification using these limits as a guide. The development team can change the limit if the chief engineer can prove that target customers do not require the specified parameters. Technical and business targets are then established top-down. The end-item target is established through market analysis. Then, major systems are allocated targets using internal expertise and key supplier input. Finally, subsystem and component targets are established using a similar process. Part of this effort includes value analysis for each major subsystem with supplier participation in a bottom-up approach to provide a check for the top-down–driven targets. Targets are then compared and rationalized as appropriate. Any team has the ability to shift around targets within its own effort as long as it meets its allocated overall target. If needed, the teams can negotiate with other teams for a larger allocation. The negotiations move up the ladder from lower to higher levels of assembly. Suppliers may be involved in target shifting negotiations within a commodity. However, they are not involved in negotiations between commodities.

Integrated suppliers have become an equal partner in the development process and are involved early in setting targets. The statement of work (SOW) is first developed internally, then reviewed and agreed on by the supplier. The commodity business plan actually calls for the company and the supplier to coplan the work. Though much information is shared, there are limits. For example, competition is so intense that cycle plans are not shared with suppliers. As a matter of fact, cycle plans often are not even shared within the company.

Ownership. A critical enabling process in supplier integration efforts is to establish ownership rights for all new technologies developed through participative efforts. This is especially critical in joint development efforts where both parties work together to develop new technologies or generate new product ideas. Successful companies address these issues up front and use appropriate mechanisms (such as patents and exclusivity agreements) to provide legal standing to their agreements. Such legal documents may be particularly important when integrating a new supplier, as the trust that can only be built over time has yet to develop.

| **Nonintegrated** | **Integrated** |

- Ownership
  —Buyer demands ownership rights to new product and process technologies

- Ownership
  —Agreement on ownership of jointly developed products and processes

CASE EXAMPLE

Phased Project Planning

This electronics company works with one of its partner suppliers to develop and prioritize a list of advanced technology programs. The companies determine the potential success of the project, resources required, and so on. They try to keep four development projects in progress at any one time. Two of the projects are generally focused on new technologies and thus have uncertain time frames and targets. One of the projects is generally focused on a specific new product development effort, and the other project may be a technology "tweak." In each case, the supplier partner has the right of first refusal to the production contract. Further, both sides maintain an intellectual property list. The standard agreement is that neither side can use or sell the other company's proprietary information without permission or reimbursement.

CASE EXAMPLE

Exclusivity

This electronics company shares technology ownership rights 50-50 with suppliers for all jointly developed technologies. However, the company requires a one-year exclusivity agreement to ensure it receives a fair return on the investment.

CASE EXAMPLE

General and Specific Contracts

This computer company uses nondisclosure agreements to protect both the company's and the supplier's interests. This agreement is defined in the company's general contract, which it signs with suppliers prior to the start of design work or any transactions. The general contract also requires suppliers to obtain permission from the company if the supplier intends to apply for a patent on technology developed as a result of the relationship with the company. This general contract will be followed with a more specific agreement if the companies actually do new product business together.

CASE EXAMPLE

Patent Rights

This chemical company indicated that patent rights are perhaps most critical in this industry because of the long new product development times (at least five years) and

(continued)

extensive investment in research and development. The company files for patent rights after the discovery process proves the viability of the product. The patent application attempts to cover a family of molecules, covering all variants that may have useful biological—and thus commercial—applications. In cases where another company has developed a potentially commercially feasible molecule but needs assistance in making the final tweaks, the company will negotiate shared patent rights with that company. The negotiation process is unique in each case, as it depends on what each company wants to get out of the process. However, the agreements generally exclude suppliers from using the technology in competing markets for a stated period of time.

Team Dynamics

Colocation. A significant change to NPD team dynamics is to strategically colocate internal team members and suppliers to support the NPD effort. Many leading companies colocate the core internal team members to facilitate communication and develop trust and ownership in the project for the duration of the project. Support team members may be colocated for the duration of their specific effort. Supplier colocation depends on the extent of involvement. Allied partners have been colocated for extensive periods of time to generate new ideas and to actually design the new product. More typically, critical suppliers have been strategically colocated for shorter periods of time to jointly conduct specific tasks such as prototyping or product qualification. Similarly, the buying firm may colocate its personnel at the buyer's site to complete specific objectives.

Nonintegrated	**Integrated**

• Colocation
    —Physically separated project teams
 	
    —Arm's length relationship with
       supplier
	• Colocation
	    —Internally colocated project team
	       personnel
	    —Supplier colocation as strategically
	       appropriate, with fostering of team
	       and partnering concepts

CASE EXAMPLE

Internal Colocation

This consumer nondurable goods company believes internal colocation of NPD team members is critical, especially as the move toward true cross-functional teams has only recently been adopted. In the absence of colocation, procurement personnel were forced to rely on research and development to keep them updated on new developments. In general, this did not work. The company's early experience is that internal colocation facilitates communication, allows for better decision making, and reduces concept-to-customer time. However, the company rarely uses supplier colocation. The company believes that because each supplier is doing something different with unique equipment and labs, there would be little to gain from supplier colocation. Selectively, the company will use supplier colocation for one to two weeks, especially in cases of codevelopment or problem resolution.

CASE EXAMPLE

Strategic Colocation

This electronics company practices supplier colocation selectively on a short-term basis. Either company may send a team over to the other's facility for up to one week. These visits are strategically selected to focus on specific stages of the NPD effort, such as prototyping. The visits may also be used to jointly resolve technical problems.

CASE EXAMPLE

Cautious Colocation

This electronics company indicates that supplier colocation is selectively used to meet strategic objectives. The supplier's design engineering group may work at the company's facility for one to two weeks at a time. The company will provide supplies, equipment, and a work area, but not salary. The primary attraction of colocation is the ease and effectiveness of communication. It is unusual to have a supplier on site that has not previously worked with the company. The frequency of colocation has increased over the last five years, but there are some concerns that may slow this trend. First, the company does not want to become too close or dependent on any single supplier, which would make it difficult to switch suppliers in the future. Second, colocation puts all proprietary information at risk, although the company indicated that it is unaware of cases in which proprietary information was actually compromised.

CASE EXAMPLE

Default Colocation

This electronics company indicates that equipment suppliers are colocated almost by default. This is because during production ramp-up of new equipment, the supplier service personnel are generally the only people capable of ensuring the equipment works as specified. On-site suppliers have access to 95 percent of the facility, so the company is particularly attentive about who is allowed on site. Suppliers must provide detailed justification for a security clearance for all on-site personnel.

Direct Communication. Another significant change to NPD team dynamics is for the buying company and the supplier to openly and directly share NPD-specific information to advance the NPD effort and resolve problems. NPD team members (this includes suppliers) must be able to openly and directly communicate with each other to ensure that accurate information is communicated and timely decisions are made. The risk is that new commitments or project changes will be made without agreements from the whole team or upper management. That is why it is so critical to ensure that team members understand what decisions they can make without review, as discussed previously.

Nonintegrated	Integrated

• Communication
  —Limited information-sharing with suppliers during new product development
  —Assign blame when problems arise, then expect the responsible party to resolve the issue
	• Communication
	  —Open and direct function-to-function communication between buyer and supplier(s)
	  —Joint identification and resolution of problems

CASE EXAMPLE

Staged Process

At this electronics company, procurement is the main point of contact throughout the supplier assessment and selection processes. However, once a supplier is selected, there is open and direct contact among and between functional levels. The reason for this staged process is to ensure that nobody, particularly engineering or research and development, makes an early sourcing decision without team consensus.

CASE EXAMPLE

Procurement Muscle

At this computer company, there are no restrictions on buyer and supplier communication, although two primary communication channels naturally emerged: engineer to engineer and procurement to procurement. The company indicated that engineer-to-engineer communication is critical to identify new technologies and advance NPD efforts. The procurement organization recently developed concerns that they were not being kept up-to-date on engineering's communication with suppliers, which led to confusion and disagreement within the company and among suppliers as to which supplier was going to be selected for integration into NPD. The procurement organization has taken proactive steps to resolve this issue. First, they notified all critical suppliers that it is in their best interests to stay in contact with procurement because procurement has significant influence not only on current but also on future sourcing decisions. Second, the procurement organization now attends all research and development and engineering staff meetings to ensure that everybody understands current issues as well as the big picture.

Learning Organization

This chemical company developed a lessons-learned database of late deliveries, unreliable materials, cost overruns, and so on. This database may be reviewed by the supplier and buyer to perform root cause analysis. The company now believes that it causes about 60 percent of the "supplier's problem." Either way, the company has established the policy of joint problem prevention, identification, and resolution. A project team works with the supplier to determine the root cause of a problem and establishes communication channels with other teams and suppliers to avoid problems on similar projects.

Language Barriers

At this company, direct function-to-function communication is used throughout the process design effort and to resolve problems as they occur. For example, with one Japanese supplier located on site, safety issues started to become a significant problem. By working together, the companies determined that information was not flowing freely nor was it understood properly because of language barriers. To resolve the problem, the company sent a number of people over to the supplier's facility in Japan to better understand equipment and processes. Further, the Japanese personnel were sent to English classes and provided with special interpreters.

Electronic Linkage

Electronic linkages are increasingly being strategically used to support the NPD effort. E-mail systems are routinely in place to facilitate communication and to transmit project documentation. Integrated CAD systems are much less prevalent across the supply base, although most companies indicated that they are linked with their allied and most critical suppliers. The two largest obstacles to widespread use of CAD systems appear to be lack of financial resources and lack of industry standards.

Nonintegrated	**Integrated**
• Limited use of linked information systems	• Increased linking information systems, both internally and externally, to support communication
• Incompatible design tools	• Increased use of aligned and linked design tools (e.g., CAD and parts databases) between buyer and supplier(s)

CASE EXAMPLE

EDI Works

This electronics company indicates that it makes widespread use of EDI to communicate business (such as schedules and forecasts) and technical (such as notice of design release) progress during the NPD effort. The main tools are voice mail, Lotus Notes, and E-mail. Despite different systems worldwide, all of these linkages follow a common process. This minimizes the need for extensive colocation. There is currently only minimal transfer of design data between companies due to technical issues. Integrated CAD systems will be used on a case-by-case basis. However, the company is integrating its technical database information to create electronic parts files accessible by internal staff and suppliers. The primary goal of this effort is to increase the use of standard parts and common building blocks in all new designs.

CASE EXAMPLE

Strategic CAD Implementation

This electronics company makes extensive use of electronic linkages to facilitate communication when face-to-face meetings are either impractical, not required, or related to noncritical and nonproprietary issues. Although the company believes face-to-face communication is best, it is not always necessary. The company has also linked its CAD systems with key suppliers, as well as with suppliers where a language barrier may exist. The key point is that like any tool, selective strategic implementation of linked CAD systems, not broad-based application, ensures success.

Leveraging

Standardization. A major change in NPD efforts is to develop and adopt NPD standards and to leverage common parts and processes to simplify development efforts. The change prevents reinventing the wheel, so that scarce resources can be allocated to those items that most add value to the final product. With a common foundation for new products, the NPD team can focus its efforts on customizing the final product to meet specific and often frequently changing customer requirements. This also minimizes the amount of new tooling and manufacturing processes required.

Nonintegrated	Integrated
• Standardization —Lack of building blocks between product generations with limited use of standard parts and processes —Designs developed without consideration of current capabilities	• Standardization —Increased use of modular designs, with increased use of standard parts and processes —Designs that consider current and future internal and supplier process capabilities

CASE EXAMPLE

Reuse Teams

This electronic company's strategic thrust is to make the back end of all of its products generic and to customize or stylize the front end for each customer line. The company has established a vision in NPD not to design each new product from scratch. It uses existing parts and building blocks to reduce costs and time to market. The company developed reuse teams to promote the use of standard building blocks and off-the-shelf application items in all NPD efforts. These teams also work with suppliers to ensure that their high-volume standard parts have the capabilities to meet the company's needs. Although supplier involvement on reuse teams is currently limited, corporate's goal is to make greater use of supplier expertise on these teams in the future. Buyers have the bulk of responsibility on reuse teams, though commodity teams provide support and input as required and ensure that different product teams are not buying duplicate items without leveraging volume buys.

CASE EXAMPLE

Industry Collaboration on Standards

This electronics company is part of an industry that is working together to develop new product standards. Customers, manufacturers, and suppliers formed an industry group that meets quarterly to review proposals and share opinions on emerging technologies and product standards. Over 250 companies are actively involved in the effort. This company felt that standards developed by the industry group have helped advance technology in new products. For example, suppliers are able to identify technology requirements early, which allows them to invest in the capabilities and capacity needed to meet their customers' goals. Further, suppliers may influence standards relevant to their products and processes.

CASE EXAMPLE

Influencing Industry Standards

This computer company tries to use as many standard components as possible in all of its new products. The current goal (which is routinely achieved) is to populate all new products with at least 90 percent standard parts. This is largely a cost saving effort, but the company indicates that through simplifying NPD efforts by limiting new parts and technologies, it also lessens the need to invest in and integrate suppliers into NPD. As a matter of fact, one of the major reasons for integrating integrated circuit suppliers is to influence industry standard components so that they include functionality important to the company's designs. The company also holds regular design reviews with external semiconductor suppliers one or two times a year. The focus of these discussions is on forecasts and standards.

CASE EXAMPLE

Supply-Base Consolidation

Even at this chemical company, which creates new molecules as a final product, there is an increasing emphasis on using existing and proven intermediates in new product development efforts. The company identifies previously designed and developed pieces or intermediates of the final product that it can now buy from suppliers to be used as building blocks for future new products. The company is also focusing on reducing from 10,000 to 5,000 the number of compounds used annually. Further, the company is increasingly only involving suppliers with proven capability to do multiple steps in the current intermediate production process and who have shown themselves able to develop innovations in support of future processes. The company has begun to optimize designs around the key supplier's capabilities and equipment. Consistent with the move toward standardization, a leadership team was assembled to consolidate the supply base, which will minimize the number of parts and increase design standardization. Standardization is also being used to take work out of managing buyer/supplier relationships, although these benefits are somewhat moderated by the amount of work required to influence supplier parts and industry standards.

CASE EXAMPLE

Standardization

Discussions at this electronics company are focused on how suppliers are responsible for developing, delivering, installing, and servicing machine tools and equipment. Suppliers are initially responsible for the maintenance of these tools, with responsibility gradually turned over to the company. Each supplier is responsible for a single process, which must be identically carried out at each of the company's major plants. Thus, when a specification or task is transferred between functions, suppliers, or new facilities, it is possible for the other party to exactly reproduce the requirements. In this way, the company leverages process standardization across the entire organization.

CASE EXAMPLE

Building-Block Technologies

This company indicates that a primary goal is to reduce the amount of customization in NPD efforts to reduce costs and cycle times. To accomplish this goal, the company will use building-block technologies to enable the group to capture systemwide cost reductions. Each building block can be packaged differently and migrated across different industrial groups (for example, industrial, automotive, and aviation). Standardization is increasingly being realized and is driving supplier integration. An in-house components engineer ensures that redesigns use standard components and are similar to existing designs. Procurement also actively analyzes new designs for potential standardization.

Systems Procurement. Another major change in NPD efforts is to increasingly shift responsibilities for higher-level assemblies and product qualification into the supply chain. This leveraging process is a natural extension of the reengineered organization and the reengineered NPD process. Supplier integration should be used to gain the greatest value added from supplier capabilities. Conducting early prototyping and testing earlier in the design process with supplier involvement has been successfully used to reduce development time and costs. Similarly, working with full-service suppliers and system-integrator suppliers has reduced cycle times and allowed buying firms to focus on their core competencies.

Nonintegrated	Integrated
• Supplier capabilities —Prototyping as the initial design nears completion —All system final assembly performed in house	• Supplier capabilities —Fast/early prototyping by and with suppliers prior to initial design completion —Allowing for system level assembly in the supply chain

CASE EXAMPLE

Early Prototyping

At this electronics company, suppliers are involved in technology development in most cases, and are integrated into specific NPD efforts to varying degrees. New technologies are assessed during an early prototype design review, which may involve multiple suppliers. The technology is tested through design verification and quality performance testing. Suppliers perform preliminary tests and predict performance before the technology is moved into a specific NPD project.

CASE EXAMPLE

The Big Picture

This chemical company indicated that it is increasingly having to show suppliers the bigger picture rather than just a small piece of the process to maximize supplier inputs. The company is posing questions more broadly to get suppliers to perform a greater share of the process. The focus is on suppliers that can perform more steps in the intermediary build-up process, while keeping final products in mind. The company is also pushing for higher involvement of suppliers in testing environmental safety and in gaining regulatory approval of new intermediates. The company is pushing higher and higher up in the compound chain and becoming more of a final assembler of the final compound or molecule. The company looks for ways to split the final molecule into commercially viable halves, for example, with different suppliers manufacturing each half.

CASE EXAMPLE

Systems Sourcing

At this automotive company, a new product planning team sets the assumptions for the new vehicle by identifying what is new, what is the latest technology, and what is to be a carryover for the program. All modules and systems are matrixed, with potential suppliers cross-referenced to this listing. Each module or system is then further broken down by subsystem, and potential suppliers are further identified. There currently may be a different supplier for each commodity. The goal of this effort is to implement system sourcing where possible. Whereas the company currently does much of the subsystem assembly internally, it may look for a supplier to act as a system coordinator to work with all the subsystem suppliers so that the company basically becomes a systems integrator. The company would do all final assembly in a plug-and-play mode. The company is driving towards common product subsystem codes to identify leverage opportunities for systems sourcing. The company is moving away from design only suppliers. Design houses have a tendency to do exactly what you want them to do, regardless of manufacturing or cost implications. A supplier with full design and production capabilities may know better. The role and responsibilities of a supplier are naturally dependent on its capabilities. The company may help develop specific supplier capabilities or provide short-term support so that the supplier can become a fully certified supplier in the long term.

Risk Management

A major change to supplier management relative to NPD is to implement sourcing strategies that build long-term commitments while still creating a sense of market competition. The goal of such a strategy is to minimize technical and business risks for both the buyer and supplier. This objective may be achieved by using a variety of mechanisms, as discussed below. The key is to have the appropriate process in place prior to execution of the NPD effort so that each party understands the ground rules before playing.

Nonintegrated	Integrated
• No contingency planning	• Joint risk/reward agreements
• Contracts periodically reopened for competitive bidding	• Long-term contracts between the buyer and supplier for the life of the developed product
• Single sourcing of product families	• Single sourcing of a part number from the supplier responsible for the design; dual sourcing within the commodity family

CASE EXAMPLE

No Guarantees

This electronics company indicated that there must be an understanding of potential outcomes and risks with integrated suppliers. For example, a supplier involved in new technology development risks the investment in significant resources without the guarantee of a production contract. Once a supplier is selected and integrated, however, the company takes the responsibility to drive market demand for the product, but makes no volume guarantees. In return for driving market demand, the company expects continuous improvement and cost reduction from the supplier, as well as assistance in the benchmarking of competitors.

The company believes cost reductions should be shared, with the supplier being allowed to keep any savings above and beyond preestablished targets. This company provides lifetime guarantees for supplied products to suppliers selected for NPD efforts. In many cases, however, the technology is changing so fast that a lifetime may be less than two years. Both the company and its suppliers expect a major technology change during the life of a project, which accelerates cost reduction and supplier competition.

The company has historically single sourced a part number, but dual sourced within a commodity family. This creates a sense of competition among suppliers while at the same time building relationships through long-term (product life) agreements. Suppliers who perform well on the current product receive favorable status for future new products. This strategy has been so effective that major OEM customers have benchmarked the process and recently adopted similar strategies.

CASE EXAMPLE

Reopener Clauses

This chemical company indicates that due to extremely high volumes, it is not likely that a single sourcing strategy can be adopted. Thus, the company typically dual sources all key materials and intermediates. However, the supplier involved or integrated early in NPD receives the bulk of business. That supplier has the right of first refusal when the molecule is required. For less critical items, or where capacity is particularly tight, the company will use a multiple sourcing strategy.

Further, this company monitors supplier performance to ensure it is receiving the highest value added and best technology available. The company attends trade shows and national industry meetings to identify state-of-the-art technology. A supplier manager internal to the company is ultimately responsible for monitoring supplier performance. Most buyer/supplier agreement have reopener clauses for poor performance,

(continued)

whether it be poor quality, service, price/cost, or technology. However, the company assures suppliers that they will not be dropped each time there is a problem.

Open Market

This consumer nondurable goods company indicated that there is no de facto assignment of business to specific suppliers. Every incumbent supplier gets the opportunity to compete for future business. However, the company believes that new technology design of material development and new product development need to be linked. Thus, development and commercialization are contractually linked. In some cases, a development competition is held. Since only one technology may be used in a product, the company informs all potential suppliers that they are competing for the technology and commercialization opportunity. When the final supplier selection decision is made, suppliers who developed technologies that were not selected are released and allowed to use those technologies however they wish.

Full-Service Suppliers

This automotive company awards suppliers integrated into new product design a production contract for the life of the specific supplied item. The company rarely works with suppliers who can only perform the design function. The company believes it is critical to link design and production.

SUMMARY

Few changes are easy and not all changes result in progress. However, strategically managed change helps overcome the obstacles through use of the proper tools and may bring a multitude of benefits to the organization.

The key to successful change is to lay the foundation by addressing the strategic issues first. For reengineering the NPD process, this means assessing and revising as appropriate the company's NPD strategy, organizational strategy, and purchasing/supply chain management strategy. The NPD strategy should focus the company on its core competencies while developing the internal skills to support these competencies. Further, the strategy must call for developing the cross-functional skills required to perform boundary spanning and identify and/or develop external suppliers that can support the company's long-term objectives.

A reengineered organization facilitates greater communication, institutes the cross-functional team concept, and allocates responsibility and authority to the proper level. It also drives continous improvement objectives throughout the organization. The reengineered purchasing/supply chain strategy drives alignment of the company's long-term goals and objectives with those of critical suppliers, and communicates to the supply base in general that the company is receptive to NPD ideas from new suppliers. These objectives may be accomplished through supplier alliances, supplier development, and long-term technology and business information-sharing with the supply base as appropriate.

With strategic issues addressed, a company may focus on the NPD execution issues. Perhaps the first key step is the formation of cross-functional NPD teams. In many cases, it is appropriate to form core teams that have cradle-to-grave responsibilities for the project. It is critical to ensure procurement's involvement on these teams, either as a core or support team member, since procurement is often most familiar with the capabilities of the supply base. It is also critical to integrate key suppliers on these teams early in the process to access their expertise and maximize their added value. Strategic use of colocation, open and direct function-to-function communication, and electronic linkages all facilitate the transmission of accurate information and timely decision making by the NPD team.

The NPD teams must be empowered to make important decisions consistent with their level of responsibility. These decisions include managing the day-to-day activities of the project, working out business and technical issues, and selecting suppliers, for example. These teams may work jointly with suppliers to develop the technical and business expectation of each party. The teams also should develop risk management strategies and understand the consequence of failure to perform.

By strategically reengineering the NPD process on both strategic and tactical dimensions, a company lays the groundwork for supplier integration to be done more efficiently and effectively. It helps prevent problems that may have occurred without the appropriate structures, strategies, and processes in place. Reengineering the NPD process provides the means to ensure that the use of internal capabilities and expertise as well as supplier capabilities and expertise is maximized.

Since supplier integration is a new process for many companies, they often have to reengineer their NPD processes to involve suppliers on the project team. For example, one company historically developed and maintained responsibility charts for NPD. However, when these charts were originally developed, the company practiced minimal outsourcing and much less supplier integration. Thus the charts are void of a supplier responsibility column. The company recognizes that understanding roles and responsibilities within a project is key, so it has revised these responsibility charts. Potential areas for supplier contribution are now listed throughout the process. Appendix 3A provides a generalized example of a reengineered new product development process, with potential procurement and supplier roles/responsibilities identified.

Appendix 3A
Reengineered Product Development Planning Chart

The following reengineered new product development planning chart identifies typical activities in a large scale development effort for a manufacturing firm. The chart is intended to focus on a supplier's or procurement's potential contribution and responsibility at each step in the process. Because of this focus, the following simplifications have been made:

- Deliverables and personnel assigned responsibility for those deliverables are not listed unless there is high potential for supplier/procurement involvement or impact.

- Planned and actual start and complete dates are not listed.

- Product design is not broken into specific disciplines (for example, electrical, mechanical, software, packaging.) The term *product design* is used to collectively reflect the design effort.

The planning chart is divided into the following stages: (1) strategic initiatives, (2) concept and program definition and approval, (3) product and process design, (4) pilot production and design verification, and (5) launch and full scale production. It is understood that successive stages of the development effort overlap to varying degrees. Many of the activities in the strategic initiatives stage are not tied to a specific new product development effort. This stage is shown, however, to reflect how procurement/supply chain management may affect long-term new product/process planning within a company. Further, it is recognized that team composition and team leadership will vary significantly between different companies and even between different projects within the same company. Therefore, the planning chart clearly must be adapted to fit a particular situation.

Legend

I. Operations		**OPER**
	A. Advanced Manufacturing	AM
	B. Manufacturing/Process or Test Engineer	MFG
	C. Quality Assurance	QA
	D. Distribution	DIS
	E. Production Scheduler/Planner	PS
II. Procurement		**PROC**
	A. Strategic/Advanced Purchasing (linked but separate from product development process)	AS
	B. Project/Product Level Purchasing	PUR
III. Engineering		**ENG**
	A. Research and Development	R&D
	B. System Engineer	SYS
	C. Design Engineer (hardware, mechanical, software)	DES
	D. Component/Materials/Maintainability/Reliability Engineer	COM
	E. Packaging Engineer	PKG
IV. Management		**MGT**
	A. Product Manager/Program Manager	PM
	B. Executive Management	EM
V. External Stakeholders		**ES**
	A. Supplier	SUP
	B. Customer	CUS
	C. Government/Agency	GVT
VI. Strategic/Support Functions		**SSF**
	A. Finance/Accounting	F/A
	B. Contracts/Legal	CON
	C. Marketing	MKT
	D. Sales	SA
	E. Technical Publications	TP
	F. Information Systems	IS
VII. Advanced Technology Teams		**ATT**
VIII. Commodity Management Team (linked but separate from NPD teams)		**CMT**
IX. New Product Development Team (composition varies depending on development stage, may include supplier)		**NPD**
X. Supplier Development Team (composition varies depending on development needs)		**SDT**

Strategic Initiatives	Lead	Procurement and Supplier's Role/Input/Issues	Supplier Deliverables
Develop overall business strategy	EM		
Define core competencies (independent of specific products)	EM	Examine if noncore competencies exist in the supply base to determine if critical commodities/capabilities will need to be developed internally or a supplier will need to be developed	
• Establish competitive business priorities	EM	Although it may vary by product, ensure cost, quality, delivery, technology, time, and flexibility trade-offs are identified, prioritized, and communicated internally and to allied suppliers	
• Identify product/process differentiators	MGT, ENG, OPER	Plan to insource differentiators or to align with key suppliers; outsource nonstrategic commodities	
• Establish insourcing/ outsourcing policy	MGT, AS	Establish and communicate decision-making policy for • Outsourcing strategic products/services • Joint development efforts • Project level make/buy decisions	
• Establish long-term design and operations capacity and capability plans	MGT, ENG, OPER	If insourcing design but outsourcing manufacture of key systems, review aligned suppliers' capabilities and capacity plans	
• Review selected allied supplier's long-term design and operation capacity/ capability plans	MGT, ENG, OPER	Ensure suppliers plan to meet your forecasted schedules, volumes, and capability requirements	
Create project structures	EM		
• Establish platform-based project development team structure	MGT	Create cradle-to-grave project team structure, identifying the potential role of a supplier on such a team	
• Implement commodity management teams	MGT	Coordinate with advanced technology teams	

79

Strategic Initiatives	Lead	Procurement and Supplier's Role/Input/Issues	Supplier Deliverables
Manage new technology development	ATT		
• Develop and maintain technology road maps	ATT	• Based on strategic business plan and core competencies • Separate technology development from specific project/product development • Jointly examine technology road maps with allied suppliers to ensure alignment • Two-way sharing of technology road maps	Technology road maps
• Solicit ideas from new suppliers	ATT, PROC, SUP	Use the Internet/WWW to link to suppliers' home pages	
• Establish technology development centers separate from product structures	ATT	• Creates single point of contact for suppliers • Facilitates decision making • Establishes confidentiality	
• Sign letters of intent with potential suppliers	MGT, ATT	• Identify business expectations (e.g., design only, design and manufacture, design with first refusal rights) • Formalize the general understanding of future expectations	
• Implement confidentiality agreements	MGT, ATT	At both the buying company and supplier	Confidentiality agreement
• Prioritize technology options	ATT, SUP	Joint meetings with allied suppliers	
• Select technologies for development	ATT, SUP	Bookshelf technologies as appropriate • Provide business assurance/letter of intent to the supplier • Release rights to nonselected technologies back to supplier	
• Develop technologies for product applications	ATT	Formalize business intentions and ownership rights	
• Transition developed technology to commodity management or product teams	ATT		

Strategic Initiatives	Lead	Procurement and Supplier's Role/Input/Issues	Supplier Deliverables
Develop procurement and supply-chain management strategies			
• Develop companywide centralized versus decentralized purchasing policy	MGT, AS	Centralized for high volume nonstrategic commodity purchases versus decentralized for strategic engineered purchases	
• Develop single source versus multiple source strategies	MGT, AS	Consider single source within a product development effort, multiple source across commodities	
• Develop global design policy	MGT, AS	Consider location of key full-service suppliers	
• Develop allied supplier partner selection and performance criteria	AS	• Emphasize long-term nonproduct specific performance criteria in both design and manufacturing capability • Provide technical training as required for procurement personnel	
• Develop full-service supplier selection criteria	AS	Emphasize medium- to long-term product specific design and operations criteria • Assess potential of suppliers to become allied partners • Allow weighting of criteria at the NPD team level • Provide technical training as required for procurement personnel	

81

Strategic Initiatives	Lead	Procurement and Supplier's Role/Input/Issues	Supplier Deliverables
• Standardize parts	AS, ENG	Create internal and external products/parts databases to support future development efforts	
• Identify system level purchasing options	AS, ENG	Assess capabilities of suppliers to take on increasing levels of responsibility for system assembly	
• Identify leverage opportunities for raw material suppliers	AS, ENG	Develop close relationships with raw material suppliers—solicit their input on new product ideas	
• Assess supply base capabilities	AS, ENG	• Use the appropriate preestablished criteria • Benchmark suppliers against the best in class	
• Identify best suppliers	AS, ENG	• Create a list of potential allied suppliers, preferred/prequalified full-service suppliers, preferred/prequalified white-box suppliers • Provide feedback to nonselected suppliers for improvement • Identify key suppliers requiring supplier development	
• Develop supply-base capabilities	AS, SDT	Establish strategy and budget for the development effort of key suppliers	Reciprocal commitment/resources to the development effort
• Rationalize supply base	AS	• Create a more manageable supply base through systems sourcing • Eliminate consistently poor performing and redundant suppliers	

Concept/Program Approval	Lead	Procurement and Supplier's Role/Input/Issues	Supplier Deliverables
Select program/project manager	EM		
Assemble concept phase core NPD team	MGT	Include allied/critical suppliers as appropriate	
Identify team training requirements	NPD	May need to focus on training for involving external sources on teams	
Identify and prioritize customer requirements (e.g., cost, quality, features)	NPD	• Solicit supplier inputs as appropriate • Learn from suppliers that have worked with competitors • Involve suppliers in QFD	
Develop and evaluate potential product/process concepts	NPD, SUP	Solicit allied supplier inputs	
Conduct concept/design competition through RFP	AS, NPD, SUP	Tools to use include insourcing/outsourcing policy and preferred supplier lists	Concept proposal
Select best product/process concept	NPD		
Select best suppliers	NPD		
Sign preliminary letters of intent with suppliers	NPD	Establish business expectations (design only, design and manufacture, design with first refusal rights, etc.)	
Finalize product concept	NPD	Input/concurrence of allied supplier	Preliminary product/process concepts Preliminary mock-up
• Model and analyze concept	ENG		
• Conduct initial ownership/legal review	CON		
• Market test concept	MKT		
Conduct preliminary risk analysis	NPD	Allied/preselected suppliers conduct their own risk analysis, which feeds overall risk analysis	Risk analysis
Concept approval	EM		

Concept/Program Approval	Lead	Procurement and Supplier's Role/Input/Issues	Supplier Deliverables
Establish system and subsystem level teams	NPD		Dedicated core personnel
Develop preliminary overall product requirements specifications/targets	NPD, SUP		• Key product/process design characteristics • Preliminary product/process description
Develop preliminary system and subsystem requirements specifications/targets	NPD, SUP	Solicit supplier input for joint development efforts	Preliminary requirements specification
Assess technologies available to meet program needs	NPD, SUP		Technology road maps
Define/assess resource requirements	NPD, SUP	Review key supplier capacity/potential readiness Includes capacity, facility, technical and human resources, tooling	Existing program/capacity plans
Develop quote packages	NPD		Quote
Select critical system and major subsystem suppliers	NPD	Based on preestablished alliance agreements	
Initiate preliminary product/process FMEA	COM		Preliminary product/process FMEA
Conduct detailed risk analysis	NPD	• Include assessment of supply risk • Consider business and technical contingency plans • Review supplier's SPC/process capability analysis	Risk assessment
Formalize program plans	NPD		
Conduct program review	NPD		
Program approval	EM		

Product and Process Design	Lead	Procurement and Supplier's Role/Input/Issues	Supplier Deliverables
Establish design phase core NPD team	PM, NPD		
Identify boundaries for information sharing with external sources	PM, NPD	Use strategic plan and core competencies as a guide	
Establish design phase system and subsystem NPD teams	PM, NPD	Identify where supplier participation is required	
Integrate preselected strategic/black-box suppliers into the appropriate NPD team	NPD	May include raw material and tooling suppliers	
• Ensure buyer and supplier top management commitment	MGT, SUP	• Management support, allocation of resources, and delegation of authority critical; direct management involvement in NPD effort not required/wanted	Letter of understanding Contractual agreement
• Integrate supplier in teams	NPD	• Periodic team meetings, direct function-to-function communication • Ensure proper personnel are involved to support current activity	
• Establish relationship manager	PM	Decision makers, key points of contact identified at each company	Identification of levels/lines of authority
• Secure confidentiality/IP agreements	PM		
• Sign technical ownership agreements	PM	Possible joint ventures	Intellectual property rights/ownership agreement
• Define roles and responsibilities	NPD	• Buying company is ultimately responsible • Must be willing to delegate authority and responsibility	Letter of understanding Statement of work

Product and Process Design	Lead	Procurement and Supplier's Role/Input/Issues	Supplier Deliverables
• Share information	NPD	• Use previously developed policies to guide level of sharing allowed/required • Review technology road maps	
• Develop design and cost targets jointly	NPD, PROC	Cost-based but market-linked pricing; allow supplier margins	Cost target agreement
• Develop design and cost performance measures jointly	NPD, DES	• Align all measures with targets • Drive for objective measures • Trade-offs between design and cost requirements clearly established • Contingency plans	Performance metrics
• Establish continuous improvement targets	NPD, DES	Value focused performance improvement goals (e.g., quality, cost, features)	Continuous improvement plan
• Agree on risk/reward sharing	NPD, CON	Address design and volume changes, economic/currency changes, and absorption of costs if full-scale production not reached	Risk/reward agreement
• Prepare mutual exit strategy	PM		
• Develop colocation strategy	NPD, DES	Determine if long-term and/or focused colocation strategy is required	Space at facility to allow for colocation personnel to allow for colocation at the buying company's site
• Establish EDI/E-mail link	IS		
• Integrate CAD/CAM system	IS		
• Link product/parts databases	IS	Facilitates standardization	Link to established parts database

Product and Process Design	Lead	Procurement and Supplier's Role/Input/Issues	Supplier Deliverables
Assess need for black/gray-box supplier design and development integration	NPD		
• Identify potential system level purchases	DES, AS, SUP	Solicit supplier inputs	
• Establish preliminary cost targets for major systems/subsystems/components	NPD, PROC	Cost-based but market-linked pricing; value engineering	
• Rate criticality of deliverables/items	NPD, PROC	Use preestablished core competency principles, strategic plan	
• Evaluate current internal design/operations capability and capacity	NPD, DES	Evaluate gaps between internal capabilities/capacity and requirements	
Select black/gray-box suppliers	NPD, PROC		
• Establish project/item specific weighted criteria for supplier selection	NPD	• Use previously established criteria as a starting point • Drive for objective measure	
• Identify potential black/gray-box suppliers	NPD, AS	Use preferred/certified supplier lists	
• Conduct RFQ	PROC		Quote
• Assess potential suppliers	NPD, PROC		
• Select suppliers	NPD, PROC	• Engineering major influence for suppliers of new technology • Drive for strong consensus • Coordinate subassembly sourcing decisions with project team	

Product and Process Design	Lead	Procurement and Supplier's Role/Input/Issues	Supplier Deliverables
Integrate black/gray-box suppliers	PM, NPD		
• Integrate suppliers	NPD	Customized product suppliers integrated early; standard part suppliers integrated later	
• Define business expectations	PM, NPD	Supplier guaranteed business (or percentage of business) unless/until it proves it is not capable	Letter of understanding Contractual agreement
• Define roles and responsibilities	PM, NPD, SUP	• Buying company ultimately responsible • Do not micromanage suppliers	Letter of understanding Statement of work
• Finalize design/cost targets	PM, CON, SUP		Cost target agreement
• Agree on performance measures	NPD, SUP		Performance metrics
Finalize design specifications	NPD, SUP	Review block-box suppliers' specification (jointly developed with gray-box suppliers)	Product/process design specifications
Product design	NPD, SUP		
• Design for standard parts	DES	Discuss building blocks/opportunities for reuse with suppliers	Analysis of standardization (parts reuse)
• DFM/DFA	DES, AM	Consider supplier capabilities	
• Order parts for engineering units/subassemblies	AS	Solicit supplier suggestions for parts most like potential final build	Parts/components for engineering builds
• Build engineering units/subassemblies	DES	Push for system assembly in the supply chain	Engineering units/mock-ups

Product and Process Design	Lead	Procurement and Supplier's Role/Input/Issues	Supplier Deliverables
• Test engineering units/subassemblies	DES	Involve suppliers in end-item testing as appropriate Supplier responsible for testing delivered items	Engineering units/mock-ups test results
• Update product FMEA	COM		Product FMEA
• Finalize key product design characteristics	DES		Key product design characteristics
• Review designs	DES		Design documentation
• Release orders for long lead time materials/components	AS		Order releases Order acceptances
• Develop manufacturing test specification	AM, SUP	Jointly establish key product test parameters	Test specification/plans
• Build/analyze design verification components	DES, SUP		• Design verification components • Design verification components test results
• Review/redline release design documents	NPD, SUP	Supplier sign-off/approval of designs for which it has major responsibility	Redline released product design documentation
• Process design	NPD, AM		
• Design for standard processes/equipment	AM, SUP		Analysis of standardization
• Plan factory layout/process routing	AM, SUP	Conduct site visits/act as a consultant where appropriate	• Process plans • Process flowcharts

Product and Process Design	Lead	Procurement and Supplier's Role/Input/Issues	Supplier Deliverables
• Design processes	AM, SUP		• Process designs • New equipment/ tooling requirements • Preliminary operator instructions
• Develop manufacturing test processes	AM, SUP		Test plans/processes
• Design test equipment	AM, SUP		Test equipment design documentation
• Update process FMEA	COM, SUP		Process FMEA
• Finalize key process characteristics	AM, SUP		• Key process characteristics • SPC analysis
• Review/redline release process design(s)	AM, SUP	Supplier sign-off/approval of designs for which it has major responsibility	Redline releases process design documentation
Tooling	AM, SUP		
• Develop tooling requirements specification	AM, SUP		Tooling requirements specification
• Integrate key tooling suppliers	AM, SUP		
• Perform tooling design	AM, SUP		Tooling design
• Review/redline release tooling designs	AM, SUP	Supplier sign-off/approval of designs for which it has major responsibility	Redline released tooling design documentation

Product and Process Design	Lead	Procurement and Supplier's Role/Input/Issues	Supplier Deliverables
• Release orders for long lead time tooling	AM, SUP		
Select white-box suppliers (make/buy decision)	NPD, PROC		
• Assess potential suppliers	PUR		
• Select potential supplier(s)	PUR		
• Develop requests for quotes	PUR		Quotes
• Select suppliers	PUR	Purchasing major influence	Letter of understanding
• Agree on performance measures	PUR		Statement of work or other contractual agreement
Conduct risk assessment	NPD	Decision to proceed with prototype build	Risk assessment

Product and Process Design	Lead	Procurement and Supplier's Role/Input/Issues	Supplier Deliverables
Prototype build and test	NPD		
• Procure prototype parts	AS		Prototype parts
• Build prototypes	AM	Integrate tooling/prototype design and build with one supplier to shrink cycle times	Prototype builds
• Verify prototype performance	DES, AM	Involve key suppliers and customers as appropriate	Prototype test results
• Update product FMEA	COM		Product FMEA
• Update process FMEA	COM		Process FMEA
Develop service/training manuals	TP		Preliminary service/training manuals
Assess supplier design performance	NPD, PROC	Measure relative to preestablished targets and metrics Use periodic milestones as well as final design milestone	
Perform risk analysis	NPD, SUP		Risk analysis
Design approved	MGT, NPD		

Pilot Production and Design Verification	Lead	Procurement and Supplier's Role/Input/Issues	Supplier Deliverables
Develop production NPD team	PM, NPD	Identify internal production team leader	Identification of production team and team leader
Order pilot production materials/components	AS		Production materials/components
Build/install/debug tooling/equipment	AM	Involve tooling suppliers in installation	
Assess internal pilot build readiness	NPD		
Assess supplier pilot build readiness	NPD, SUP		Released/controlled program plans
• Assess supplier process design	AM		
• Review supplier product/process FMEA	COM		
• Assess supplier performance measures	QA		
Blueline release all product/process design documentation	NPD, SUP	Supplier sign-off/approval of designs for which it has major responsibility	Blueline released product/process design documentation
Conduct pilot build	NPD, SUP		
• Train production workers	MFG		Internal training
• Verify internal processes	MFG		
• Verify supplier processes	MFG, QA		Joint and/or self-audit report

Pilot Production and Design Verification	Lead	Procurement and Supplier's Role/Input/Issues	Supplier Deliverables
• Build key customer pilot units	MFG		Pilot units
• Sample test pilot with key customers	MKT		
• Build key supplier pilot units	MFG		Pilot units
• Sample test pilot with key suppliers	AS		Pilot test report
• Build qualification units	MFG		Qualification units
• Test qualification units	COM		Qualification unit test report
• Verify/update reliability data	COM		
• Update/rerelease design documentation as required	NPD, SUP		Updated/rereleased design documentation as required
Update process FMEA	COM		Process FMEA
Update product FMEA	COM		Product FMEA
Assess supplier performance	NPD, SUP		
Perform risk analysis	NPD, SUP		Risk analysis
Decision to proceed to launch	**MGT**		

Launch and Full-Scale Production	Lead	Procurement and Supplier's Role/Input/Issues	Supplier Deliverables
Verify supplier production readiness	MFG	Conduct on site audits	Pilot production post audit
• Review supplier QA plans	QA		
• Review supplier production plans	MFG		
Update/release production schedules	OPER, SUP	Finalize/communicate production forecasts/plans	Production schedules
Build and test initial production units	MFG		Initial production units
Evaluate internal processes	NPD		
• Monitor process capability/control	QA, MFG		
• Drive continuous process improvement	QA, MFG		
• Assess product/component quality	QA, MFG		

Launch and Full-Scale Production	Lead	Procurement and Supplier's Role/Input/Issues	Supplier Deliverables
Assess supplier performance	NPD	Involve suppliers if problems arise	
• Evaluate quality of purchased parts	QA		
• Evaluate delivery time of purchased parts	PUR		
Service customers after sales	QA	Involve suppliers as appropriate	Customer service
• Assess product performance complaints	QA		
• Repair/service products	QA		
• Evaluate warranty claims	QA		
• Perform failure analysis	QA		
• Implement corrective action	QA		
Identify process improvements	QA, MFG	Solicit supplier inputs on internal and supplier process improvements	Process improvement plans
Identify product improvements	QA, MFG	Solicit supplier inputs on internal and supplier product improvements	Product improvement plans
Publish lessons learned report	QA	Allow supplier access to relevant portions of internal database	Lesson learned database

Chapter 4

Establishing Current and Future Needs

Suppliers are like fish in the ocean. We [the buyers] are the fishermen. The key challenge facing us is how to put out the right bait, so that we can pull up the right suppliers at the right time and get them to help us develop our products. There are several problems associated with fishing: How do we know we're using the right bait? How do we know the right kind of fish are in the water? Most importantly, when we catch a fish, how do we know whether it's the right fish, and whether we should keep it or throw it back in the water? Finally, how do we know the fish will follow through with its commitments if we decide to keep it?

Product development manager from computer manufacturer describing
the integration of suppliers into the new product development process

INTRODUCTION

The above metaphor illustrates the problems associated with supplier evaluation and selection for integration into the new product development cycle. The best companies examined in this project integrated suppliers early in the product concept stage of the new product development cycle. These companies had formal processes that assessed internal and external product or process technology requirements, costs, and supplier capabilities based on a team decision. All of the companies realized the importance of the decisions that occur prior to the integration of suppliers: a comprehensive assessment of the need for supplier expertise in a given technology as well as the alignment of the buying organization with the supplier for future projects.

Several trends are driving companies to rely more on external collaboration with suppliers for new product/process/service technologies.[1] The pace of technology and product development has increased dramatically, and the effective transfer of technology in a timely manner has become an increasingly critical success factor. Concurrently, the cost and complexity of new technology development has continued to increase, and technology venturing and partnering has emerged as a major threat to maximizing commercial opportunities and technology's value. The role of the research and development function is

---

[1]Ronald S. Jonash, "Strategic Technology Leveraging: Making Outsourcing Work for You," *Research-Technology Management,* March–April 1996, 19–25.

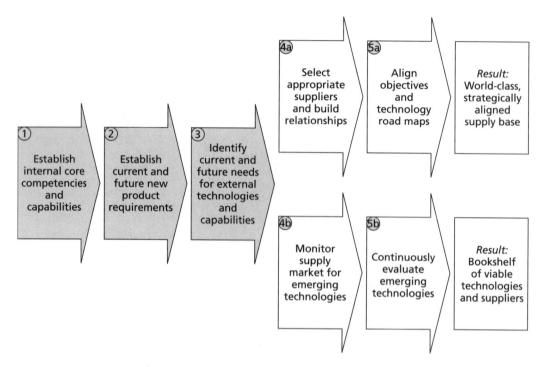

Figure 4.1. Supplier integration strategic planning process.

therefore placing less focus on managing the function, and more on generating and leveraging technology value for the company. Integration of external source of technology results in acceleration of technology commercialization, improved cost-effectiveness, stronger technology competencies, and a greater scope of technology reach and customer intelligence.

In order to derive such benefits, however, companies must have a formal supplier integration strategy that is undertaken as part of the company's overall competitive strategy. Companies must put in place a systematic process to ensure that they make the best competitive use of internal core competencies and that they have external access to the capabilities and technologies that will properly complement their internal core competencies over the long term. As mentioned in Chapter 2, this process consists of three major elements, broken down into seven steps (see Figure 4.1):

- Determining current and future needs

    1. Establish internal core competencies and capabilities

    2. Establish current and future new product requirements

    3. Identify current and future needs for external technologies and capabilities

- Developing a well-aligned world-class supply base

    4. Select appropriate suppliers and build relationships

    5. Align objectives and technology roadmaps

- Developing a bookshelf of viable technologies and suppliers
  6. Monitor supply market for emerging technologies
  7. Continuously evaluate emerging technologies

In this chapter, we discuss in detail the first three stages of the process. These stages focus on the insourcing/outsourcing decision regarding design and manufacturing and how the best companies are able to reach a consensus on this decision. Clearly, no single company is likely to have sufficient expertise in all of the technologies required to effectively internalize design and production.

In this first stage of the process, companies identify the core competencies to keep within the company, determine what technologies will be required in future new products, and relate these requirements to future planning for external technology needs. In this chapter, we go through each of these steps in detail and describe the subprocesses and relevant criteria used in the best companies interviewed in our study. We also provide illustrative details from the case studies to facilitate understanding of the process.

In Chapter 5, we will provide details on the consensus-building process used in evaluating supplier capabilities and deciding which suppliers to use. An important part of this process is the quality of the buying company's performance assessment process, which serves as the primary information input into the supplier selection decision. We will identify a number of specific performance criteria used in evaluating suppliers. Once suppliers are selected, the best companies also seek to align core suppliers with their future technology strategies in order to improve future information sharing and communication processes. In some cases, this includes formalized risk/reward sharing agreements to explicitly identify what each party can expect from the relationship. The outcome of this stage of the process is a world-class supply base positioned to meet the company's future product requirements.

Chapter 6 examines the effective management of technological risk associated with the external sourcing decision. Many companies try to manage technological risk by monitoring the development of new technologies and, for those technologies that appear to have promising applications, manage their introduction in new product applications so as to balance the benefits of "first mover" status with the risks of the technology. The objective is to maintain a selection of promising technologies on the bookshelf and for the technologies to be at an acceptable level of maturity when the company wants to use them in a new product application.

DETERMINING CURRENT AND FUTURE NEEDS: AN OVERVIEW

Across all the companies visited, the design/manufacturing decision is being subjected to a much more thorough analysis than in the past. The best companies have a systematic process in place for defining the level and types of commodities for which the insourcing/outsourcing decision is to be made. Whenever possible, companies are approaching the outsourcing decision from a systems perspective and are asking suppliers to increase their responsibility for subsystem integration. This was observed to be the case for a variety of

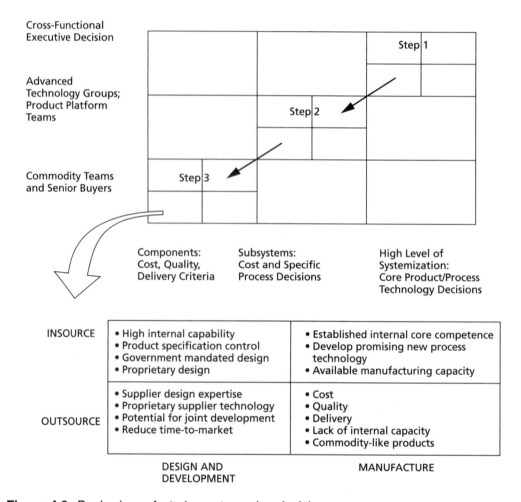

Figure 4.2. Design/manufacturing outsourcing decision process.

products and processes, including chemical molecules, automobiles, installation and maintenance of new processes, and computer components.

The decision-making process begins at a high systemization level, which assesses strategic core competencies in product and process design and manufacture (see Figure 4.2). At this level, the unit of analysis involves decisions regarding core technologies, system integration, and which technologies to commit resources to in order to develop them internally. Generally speaking, we observed a trend towards outsourcing commodity-like items and focusing internal efforts on added-value activities such as system integration. In all of the companies, this decision was made at higher levels in the organization, as it involved a strategic statement regarding where the company is headed over the next 10 to 20 years.

Once consensus is reached, executives formalize the strategy and communicate it to the divisions, which are then responsible for establishing current and future new product requirements (step 2). The process of cascading this decision to the next level of decision making is achieved through a variety of means. One of the major organizational structures employed to interpret and deploy these strategies is the advanced technology group. These groups are typically centrally located and are tasked with identifying major new subsystem and component technologies required in new products. Another approach involves integration of suppliers into process development and start-up. Some companies use institutionalized platform teams responsible for new product development with suppliers on a permanent basis. Finally, other companies employ a letter of intent that formally specifies the nature of the relationship. The decision making at this stage is typically done by product development teams, using the executive core competence assessment as a guiding vision.

Finally, in step 3, decisions regarding specific insourcing/outsourcing at the component level are typically made at the senior buyer or commodity team level. Key evaluation criteria for these decisions include cost, quality, ramp-up, delivery, and performance criteria. Purchasing is responsible at this level for identifying leading suppliers within a commodity class and sharing this information with the commodity team. In some cases, however, the decision may be made independent of a commodity team. In the following pages, we provide examples of companies and how they implement each of these three stages of the process.

STEP 1—ESTABLISH INTERNAL CORE COMPETENCIES AND CAPABILITIES

Across all the organizations, the level of item for which the determination of core competencies is made varies tremendously—from molecules to facilities. This variation reflects the many different types of industries and products assessed in the study. Despite the difference in product type, a number of common themes emerge in how companies assess their internal core competencies and decide to insource or outsource an item.

Because of the strategic importance of the insourcing/outsourcing decision and its relationship to the core competence of an organization, the decision (particularly at the systems level) should be made at higher levels in the organization and cascaded down to the firm/strategic business unit level. Several criteria are used to identify core competencies, depending on industry and market characteristics. The best companies have conducted an exhaustive and comprehensive analysis of this decision before proceeding to the next decision-making phase. The major variables considered in the core competence decision include:

- Internal engineering capabilities and intellectual property

- Manufacturing capabilities and capacity

- Ability to meet target costs

- Market conditions

- Current and future potential of product/process technology for achieving a competitive advantage

- Availability of qualified sources

- Potential for standardization and leveraging
- Ability to meet quality requirements

The nature of these variables typically depends on industry and company characteristics.

CASE EXAMPLE

Single and Multiple Source

One automotive manufacturer typically single sources by product platforms but uses multiple suppliers across the corporation. The company has a high level of systemization, sourcing large components and discouraging microsourcing. A set of materials is first approved, and suppliers are allowed to manage the second tier. Target costs are established at the assembly/module level, but with a large degree of devolved management of cost to the first-tier supplier.

Insourcing/outsourcing decisions are made based on acknowledged core competencies. In this company, engines and bodies are considered core, and any other part that is not vehicle-specific is considered not core. Body styling is an intellectual property, which is considered core, although the design of the style is not considered core. However, this continues to be the subject of much debate. In most cases, an executive management committee makes the decision about what is to be outsourced, independent of any product, and the decision is handed down to the purchasing team at the division, which is largely responsible for supplier selection and integration. In this manner, the core competency decision is essentially handed off to the product platform team.

CASE EXAMPLE

Don't Duplicate Capabilities

Another automotive manufacturer has a new product development process that corresponds to a four-year development cycle, with key products being initiated every second year. This cycle essentially institutionalizes supplier involvement, which the company has been doing since the earliest days of its inception. This company's product development process is differentiated by the level of control and integration of suppliers into the process. The company has become very proficient at target costing internally and has also developed a very high internal design capability. Corporate executives feel there is no need to duplicate capabilities externally and internally. As a result, purchasing controls the role of the supplier much more carefully, and the company does much less external supplier design, or black-box, than other automotive companies.

The manufacturing outsourcing decision is therefore much more of a cost decision, in which a system of checks and balances between research and development and purchasing is used to analyze supplier-submitted cost estimates. The company has also designed a hierarchy of part competencies, which identify

- Internal versus external competencies
- Company versus competitor competencies
- Market conditions
- Imitation and application

Typically, internal manufacturing competencies include engine assemblies, selected unique processes (such as engine machining), final assembly, welding, side panels, and so on. External manufacturing is used for noncritical items and some machining.

CASE EXAMPLE

Insource Strategic Manufacturing Requirements

One consumer products manufacturer only insources manufacturing that is strategic in nature. Components, subassembly, and other nonproprietary processes that are not strategic in nature are outsourced. This decision is made at the product supply/general management level. The company recognizes that there is a critical need for better/more objective methods for the make or buy decision. The company has recently diverted from a vertical integration focus and uses rate of return and net present value figures as hurdles in the make or buy decision. In addition, the company is attempting to emphasize performance specifications instead of physical property specifications. This change in focus is creating a number of difficulties for research and development, which must now identify these performance specifications very early in the product development cycle.

CASE EXAMPLE

Outsource Assembly

Computer companies are also recognizing the importance of the insourcing/ outsourcing decision, so that the decision-making process is occurring at executive levels. This is particularly true for one manufacturer of personal computers. This company has recognized that computer assembly is no longer a value-added process, and narrow margins are forcing manufacturers to rethink the issue of core competence. The company therefore is seeking to keep commodities outside of the company and is focusing on process differentiation as part of its insourcing/outsourcing strategy.

CASE EXAMPLE

Establish Core Competence

Another computer company has also established a companywide strategy to establish what will be designed and manufactured in-house. Again, a business plan is developed at the highest level in the company, and is then filtered down into plans for each of the

(continued)

product groups. The company has recognized that its core competence lies in the area of system integration and system testing, not in component manufacture. Therefore, it expects technology breakthroughs from selected suppliers. For this reason, it is constantly communicating with suppliers, who provide leading-edge information on new technology developments and market needs. The reliance on technology is so great that a solid supplier relationship may be dissolved to pursue a relationship with a more technologically advanced supplier, even though the current supplier may be performing well on quality and cost.

CASE EXAMPLE

Outsourcing Molecules

A chemical manufacturer considers portions of molecules as building blocks in assessing supplier competence. The company's strategy is to accelerate the rate of new product development by focusing on fewer compounds annually and integrating suppliers who have proven capabilities and can perform multiple steps in the intermediate product process. Instead of asking suppliers to supply basic elements only, the company is actively asking suppliers how to make the intermediate molecules with the final molecules in mind. This involves showing them a bigger picture (not just a small piece of the process), posing the question more broadly, and getting the supplier to perform a greater share of the process. Supplier integration is facilitated by having broader secrecy agreements to cover more issues as the supplier gains access to more pieces of the molecule puzzle. In some cases, the company even licenses parts of molecules from university research centers. The strategy driving this integration is to push higher up the compound chain, becoming more of an assembler of the final compound or molecule.

Across these companies, a variety of criteria are used in determining which products and processes should be outsourced, depending on the industry and the company. Although the criteria vary, we found a great deal of commonality in the processes used to arrive at the decision.

STEP 2—ESTABLISH CURRENT AND FUTURE NEW PRODUCT REQUIREMENTS

In all of the companies previously described, a structured vision is created by top-ranking executives regarding defined areas of expertise considered to be a core competence. Following this step, decisions made at the executive level are handed down to product-level teams/divisions, which use the overall core competence decisions and interpret them at a product level. These groups also identify patterns in market shifts, emerging technologies, customer requirements, and industry trends to help identify a product-level technology strategy regarding current and future requirements. This helps transition the technology decisions from a broad systems to a subsystems level.

A critical part of planning for new product development is figuring out what features and performance capabilities will be wanted/needed by customers, and when. This requires a clear understanding of the target market as well as an understanding of currently available and developing technologies that might be applied to meet customer needs. The decision of whether and when to introduce a new feature or technology often involves balancing customer desires, cost, and the maturity or riskiness of a new technology.

CASE EXAMPLE

Commodity/Supplier Matrix

Early in its new product development process, one automotive company assigns a pre-program team, which identifies the assumptions for the new vehicle by identifying what is new, what is the latest technology, and what is to be a carryover. The team then creates a matrix identifying the commodities and potential suppliers. For example, the matrix rows may include items such as brakes, suspension, and drive train, while columns list potential suppliers. Each commodity is then further broken down by subsystem and potential suppliers are identified for each. For example, brakes may be broken down into booster, foundation brakes, master cylinder, and so on, with suppliers identified for each.

CASE EXAMPLE

Integrate Customer Requirements

In one division of a Japanese company that manufactures personal and commercial communication equipment, only a few key parts are supplied by internal divisions, with the remainder outsourced. Customer requirements are integrated into the development cycle at the feasibility study stage. Marketing submits these requirements based on its research, and engineers judge whether they are technically feasible. If the technology is available, the cost/value relationship must be assessed before making a final decision to incorporate the feature.

STEP 3—IDENTIFY CURRENT AND FUTURE NEEDS FOR EXTERNAL TECHNOLOGIES AND CAPABILITIES

The final issue involved in determining current and future needs is a decision regarding the necessary/desired level of supplier involvement. An important part of institutionalizing supplier integration is separating advanced technologies from standard technologies and deciding on the appropriate level of supplier integration. Procurement must work closely with other functional groups to carry out its key role in this process.

None	White Box	Gray Box	Black Box
No supplier involvement. Supplier "makes to print."	Informal supplier integration. Buyer consults with supplier on buyer's design.	Formalized supplier integration. Joint development activity between buyer and supplier.	Design is primarily supplier driven, based on buyer's performance specifications.

Increasing Supplier Responsibility →

Figure 4.3. Spectrum of supplier integration.

CASE EXAMPLE

Put It in Writing

One Japanese electronics firm states directly in its purchasing policy manual that purchasing must "always maintain close relationships with the manufacturing, technical, and sales departments to understand their trends in advance, and to strive to acquire the needed information and knowledge."

The level of supplier integration can vary along a continuum, ranging from none (supplier makes to print) to black box (where the supplier has nearly complete responsibility for both design and manufacture of the component). This is shown in Figure 4.3. In practice, most integration efforts seem to be gray box, where joint development of a component/product occurs.

One of the most important drivers for making this decision is the segmentation of different technologies in order to identify and attract potential suppliers that have the technological expertise that does not reside internally. Many of the companies we studied have developed advanced technology groups tasked specifically with identifying new technologies and suppliers.

CASE EXAMPLE

Blue Sky/Reuse/New Product Teams

One electronics company we studied has segmented its purchasing organization into three key groups and has carefully defined how supplier involvement with each group occurs. The first group consists of blue sky advanced technology centers tasked with long-range thinking looking 5 to 10 years out into the future. Commodity teams in this group are responsible for 100 percent of the needs and must therefore know the industry, be aware of changes in commodity markets, gain access to the technology road maps of suppliers, and share that information internally. Any supplier involvement that occurs with this group focuses on technology and not specific product requirements (although the technology will eventually support specific requirements).

A second set of procurement groups are the reuse teams, responsible for promoting the use of standard, shelf application items over a 1-year to 5-year planning horizon. Individual buyers make sourcing decisions for 75 percent of needs in this category, while commodity teams make decisions for the remaining 25 percent. Executives have identified the need for greater supplier involvement on the reuse teams.

The final category of procurement groups is the new product development program teams involved in specific applications in which the company has won business over a 2-year planning horizon. Buyers are responsible for 100 percent of these teams' needs. These are very focused teams, as they address specific customer requirements that need to be met. The teams use a five-phase new product development process with reviews after each stage. Executive management is also seeking to promote active integration directly with suppliers during development. A key measure driving this process is the percentage of reuse by the program teams.

CASE EXAMPLE

Engineering Fellows

In an industrial controls company, a key component of new product strategy is the ability to leverage the knowledge of suppliers in the new product development effort. The new product development area is composed of 260 people. New products are organized around different customer sets. Engineering fellows within each of the divisions are responsible for ensuring that new technologies are indeed state of the art. The primary basic new technology center is in the corporate headquarters; this group is responsible for infusing new technologies and scanning markets, and it communicates via a technology council staffed in part by personnel from this division. However, divisional groups carry out all of the real product development work. The new product development process was reengineered two years ago, so many of the processes are still being implemented. The process consists of three stages:

1. Strategic initiative plan—research, generate, validate

2. New product development—planning, concept, design, production

3. New product introduction—development, prelaunch, postlaunch

The strategic initiative plan is really where the decision on the level of supplier integration is made. At this stage, the team asks itself: "Do we have a supplier with a

(continued)

core competency in this area, or do we need to develop a new supplier?" All potential suppliers are considered. Purchasing is responsible for making the final decision regarding the supplier to use.

The level of involvement of the supplier may vary substantially from one project to the next. The company typically relies on suppliers more for their process technology than for their product technology. Suppliers are often brought in early and sit in on the customer negotiation meeting. This is done so that suppliers understand the total design earlier and have an opportunity to influence the design. In this case, the functional specs are defined, and suppliers work with the company to jointly ensure the specs are met.

CASE EXAMPLE

Overlapping Product Life Cycles

Due to relatively short product life cycles, one computer company we studied may be marketing three to four generations of products simultaneously, all at different points in the product life cycle. Sourcing strategies will differ at these different stages. For growing and mature products, multiple sourcing may be used to ensure capacity requirements. Major changes have occurred in this company's insourcing/outsourcing decisions, with the trend being towards more outsourcing. This trend is largely a function of improved supplier quality. Increased supplier size has also contributed to this trend, though the overall number of suppliers in this market has been reduced dramatically. To facilitate this change, the company has focused on supplier development and has increasingly disclosed reliability improvement processes to its suppliers in order to help the suppliers improve their quality.

Laboratory work is an important first step in the process. The lab is responsible for developing technologies that are put on the bookshelf. Technologies may be developed internally or jointly with suppliers and are brought on line when mature. Cross-functional teams are involved throughout. However, the composition of the core team depends on the stage of development. A project team is formed before new product planning and initially consists of design engineering, manufacturing engineering, and marketing. Procurement is typically not directly involved until the prototype design phase.

Suppliers are integrated into this process to varying degrees. To increase the probability of success, several suppliers may be directly involved in the technology development. The company's design team provides performance specifications to the supplier, which then develops a detailed design to meet the specifications. For technologies that are relatively well-established, multiple suppliers may be approached with developed specifications. The company will support development activity while several suppliers are working simultaneously on a design without a contract.

CASE EXAMPLE

From Dirt to Finished Product

Another company in the electronics industry involves suppliers in a rather unique way when it sets up new plants. The company's objective is to get factories from dirt to finished product in less than two years. To further this objective, the company involves suppliers to facilitate quicker ramp-up of new facilities.

There are literally hundreds of machine tools in a given facility. The company holds suppliers responsible for delivering, installing, servicing, and maintaining the machine tools, which may cost well over a million dollars each. This involves suppliers in process ramp-up and maintenance of equipment in the facilities. While the company also involves suppliers in new product development, process integration represents a truly unique application in a nontraditional area. Suppliers are first fully responsible for the maintenance of these machine tools, and the maintenance tasks are then gradually turned over to internal people. Each supplier is responsible for a single process, which is identically carried out at its three facilities in different parts of the world. The company emphasizes the replication of processes across all facilities. The mandate is that any time a specification or task is transferred between functions or suppliers, the other party is responsible for exactly reproducing the requirements.

SUMMARY

After completing the first three stages of the strategic process, companies should have identified a vision statement regarding the company's internal core competencies, established a set of requirements for success in current and future new products, and have a general idea of the technology needs within these product groups. In addition, the company should have a general idea of the specific roles and responsibilities it wishes to place on suppliers selected for new product development. Companies should seek to formally specify these objectives in as much detail as possible, since in the next three stages, they become the primary criteria used in supplier selection, negotiation, alignment, and relationship management.

Chapter 5

Establishing a Strategically Aligned World-Class Supply Base

"One of our biggest challenges in working with suppliers is maintaining a high level of trust after the first two year 'honeymoon' period is over."

Fortune 500 purchasing executive

INTRODUCTION

Once a company has established *what* its current and future needs for external technologies and capabilities are, it must address the issue of *who* will fulfill these needs. This chapter focuses on selecting suppliers who have or can develop the capabilities to meet the buying company's current and future needs, building relationships with those suppliers, and ensuring that the suppliers' objectives and technology plans are well-aligned with the buying company's needs over the long term (Figure 5.1).

Several key points are evident in considering the strategies companies use in selecting and building relationships with suppliers for integration into new product development. Before a supplier is integrated, a decision must be made about the pool of available suppliers, which of these are the best suppliers, and what type of relationship should be established. This decision should be made by a cross-functional group that includes, at a minimum, engineering and purchasing personnel. Investing sufficient time and resources in supplier selection and alignment has paid off for the most successful companies. We found that, over time, companies using prequalified suppliers with which the company had previous experience were more likely to be successful in their integration efforts than companies using new, unqualified suppliers.

The generic process map in Figure 5.2 provides an overview of the tasks associated with developing a well-aligned, capable supply base. Three important points should be recognized in considering this process. First, companies should be aware of the fact that supplier selection systems that only consider existing suppliers may be overlooking potential sources of innovation and/or cost savings. Purchasing can play a key role in constantly scanning the environment (both within and outside of the industry) for potential new suppliers who are developing new product and process technologies that may offer significant

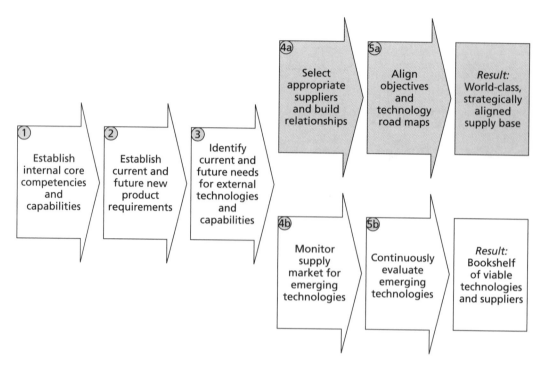

Figure 5.1. Supplier integration strategic planning process.

innovation and/or cost savings. Second, if supplier integration is to be a successful long-term strategy, finding capable suppliers is a first step, which must be followed up by making sure that the supplier's future plans align well with the buying company's future needs. Finally, establishing a well-aligned world-class supply base does not eliminate the need to carefully manage the execution of each individual integration effort.

STEP 4A—SELECT APPROPRIATE SUPPLIERS AND BUILD RELATIONSHIPS

The best companies employ a systematic and thorough assessment of key suppliers, driven by the use of cross-functional commodity teams, which helps improve supplier capabilities and inputs over time. Companies employ a commodity team structure designed to enable a global search for the best worldwide suppliers in any given commodity group. Commodity team consensus, particularly between engineering and purchasing, is a critical part of this process. A variety of different performance criteria are used in assessing suppliers, going beyond the usual criteria considered in selecting ordinary material or service suppliers. Finally, partnership or alliance relationships are often established with suppliers who are to be heavily involved in new product development efforts.

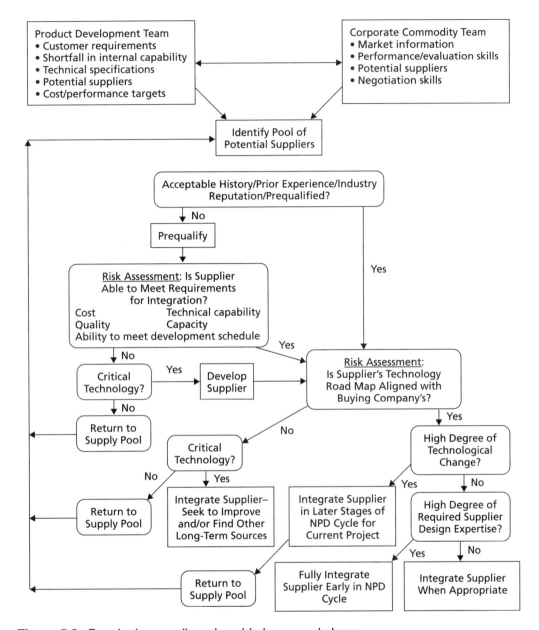

Figure 5.2. Developing an aligned world-class supply base.

Cross-Functional Commodity Management Structures

The best companies we examined employ a detailed commodity management structure that facilitates the interaction between technology and purchasing personnel. This interaction permits the input of both parties in performing both a technical evaluation and a market-based evaluation on the relative merits and problems associated with integrating a given supplier. The following examples illustrate some of the different types of commodity management structures that can be used successfully.

We Can't Do It Alone

This electronics company made a major organizational switch from procurement strategy boards to product-focused commodity teams in 1992. At this point, purchasing gave up some dominance (buyers gave up sole responsibility for sourcing), yet it was recognized that the teams still needed supplier evaluation and selection skills. This switch reflected the belief that engineering could no longer continue to invent the future, but needed to rely more on suppliers to do so. Commodity teams are tasked with focusing on those suppliers that targeted the automotive industry and on suppliers who were open and clear about their strategic focus. Part of this task involved considering capacity, total cost, and technology criteria and ensuring that different product teams do not duplicate effort by separately buying common or duplicate items. In general, the team is also responsible for supplier development and intimately understanding the commodity. This change was formally stated using four global guiding principles:

- Develop common practices across businesses
- Be a global company that uses suppliers from around the world
- Leverage resources
- Source at the site of design for custom parts

The initial departure point for a given commodity team is with the commodity technology road map. This road map is a key linkage between the commodity strategy and product technology strategy. In general, commodity teams are expected to conduct a worldwide search for the best suppliers. One manager noted that in order to really drive technology, you must also team up with a company that has technology from around the globe. In general, the company has encountered no particular barriers in using European companies, with standard intellectual property safeguards. However, with Japanese suppliers, language often becomes a barrier to communication between engineering groups. Many Japanese suppliers have established U.S. centers because of the barriers posed by distance and language.

A good example of a commodity team in action involves a negotiation with a European supplier who was selected after ten suppliers presented their design for a new project. The presentations were formally evaluated quantitatively by the commodity team. During the course of the selected supplier's presentation, the team found it could satisfy its requirements with an off-the-shelf chip set from the supplier. The team visited selected supplier facilities, and the supplier sent a team to the United States during the course of the project. The commodity team also works in parallel with other commodity teams on the product development group.

A key element in the structure of these teams is that it is not a 100 percent engineering-led process, even though engineering has traditionally dominated decisions. The new vision is to retain a core set of knowledge to respond to end customer needs and to develop more interfaces with suppliers to identify which technologies can meet the requirements. The company cannot afford to be shut out of a new technology, so the group must constantly be transferring knowledge from a variety of sources, including customer requirements, aftermarket (where new technologies often show up first), trade shows, competitive assessments, and alliances.

CASE EXAMPLE

A Full-Time Job

At one computer manufacturer, the core new product development team is headed by a development engineer who is a full-time project manager, and also includes materials/procurement, design, marketing, systems engineers, and operations planning. Between five and eight materials representatives work with the respective commodity teams to select suppliers and identify needs from those suppliers. The materials organization has approximately 40 commodity teams, which must interface efficiently with the core program teams that develop 40 or more new products a year. This is sometimes problematic, as the new product development teams are divisional, while materials is situated at the corporate level.

CASE EXAMPLE

Ringi—Management by Consensus

One Japanese company has a long history of focusing on procurement and supplier management as a key competitive strategy. An important component of Japanese new product development strategies is the importance of *Ringi,* or management by consensus. All decisions are made via cross-functional consensus of multiple individuals. This process is an inherent part of Japanese culture. Issues are discussed exhaustively in both formal and informal settings before a decision is reached. This technique is very good for reaching a consensus and making a decision that everyone can live with. However, Japanese executives are quick to point out that this process takes much longer, which can be a problem when product development cycles must be reduced.

CASE EXAMPLE

Making the First Cut

In the personal and commercial communication equipment division of this same company, only a few key parts are supplied by internal divisions, with the remainder out-

(continued)

sourced. In the first stage of supplier integration into new product development, the team filters suitable candidates for design and development. Engineering and purchasing jointly select suppliers, but engineering plays the stronger role in the decision. Engineering performs a technical evaluation of the potential suppliers, and purchasing handles final contract negotiations. Site visits by engineering and purchasing personnel are used to evaluate both manufacturing and engineering capability of the supplier. Cost, quality, delivery performance, and the supplier's technical capability are the main considerations in supplier selection. Previous new product development involvement is also a major factor in evaluating suppliers.

Supplier Assessment Criteria

A set of specific performance measures related to customers' needs and requirements should be used to reach a consensus on a potential supplier's capabilities and subsequent selection. Cost, quality, and delivery are, of course, relevant, but evaluating suppliers for potential integration into new product development should involve criteria beyond those used to evaluate ordinary material/service suppliers. Based on the experience of the companies studied, the following elements are likely to be important in considering new or existing suppliers for integration:

- Targets: Is the supplier capable of hitting affordable targets regarding cost, quality, and product performance/function (such as weight, size, and speed)?

- Timing: Will the supplier be able to meet the product development schedule?

- Ramp-up: Will the supplier be able to increase capacity and production fast enough to meet volume production requirements?

- Innovation and technical expertise: Does the supplier have the required engineering expertise and physical facilities to develop an adequate design, manufacture it, and solve problems when they occur?

- Training: Do the supplier's key personnel have the required training to start required processes and debug them?

All of the above criteria must be tied into the evaluation/measurement system in order to develop a comprehensive risk assessment that answers the following questions:

- What is the likelihood that this supplier has the ability to bring the product to market?

- How does this risk compare to other potential suppliers (if there are others)?

- At what point are we willing to reverse this decision if we proceed, and what are the criteria/measures for doing so?

- What is the contingency plan that takes effect in the event the supplier fails to perform?

We will provide examples of the different types of assessment criteria, and how companies go about determining relative supplier capabilities in each area. Many of these dimensions are difficult to assess without direct experience with the supplier. The companies we studied showed a strong preference for integrating suppliers with whom they had prior experience.

Performance Targets. Almost every company had some sort of system that assessed the supplier's ability to meet different performance targets. Target costing was employed at almost every company prior to supplier selection. Other performance targets included quality, technical specifications, delivery, and evidence of continuous improvements occurring within the supplier's organization. Note that many companies still employ market testing prior to supplier integration in order to investigate whether an existing supplier is truly providing a competitive price and is capable.

CASE EXAMPLE

Supplier Report Cards

At one company, supplier selection processes and measurement systems are all handled through strategic supply. Once a commodity strategy is established and the supplier selection/negotiation process is complete, control of the decision switches to the acquisition group from strategic sourcing. Anytime a product enters the product release point, a transition occurs, and supplier management becomes the responsibility of the acquisition group. Currently, 85 percent of the top-dollar suppliers receive a supplier report card. The company is in the process of significantly reducing the supply base. This is being carried out by individual buyers in coordination with manufacturing. For instance, the company has reduced 53 stamping suppliers down to 3. There is also considerable effort devoted to cycle-time reduction through joint work with corporate information systems and accounts payable groups in implementing EDI.

CASE EXAMPLE

The Four Cs

At another company, a major initiative in supplier capability management is the C4 continuous improvement process. The process focuses on the four Cs:

- Commitment to quality

    —DPM, PPM, and EPM measurements

    —Statistical controlled processes

    —Design for quality

    —Ship-to-stock

    —Cost of quality

    —ISO 9000 certified

    —Malcolm Baldrige National Quality Award qualification

(continued)

- Cycle-time reduction
  —Lead-time reduction in production and tooling

  —Elimination of non–value-added tasks in production and administration

  —Early supplier involvement at the design stage

  —Tactical techniques (forecasting, kanban, EDI, in-house support, process mapping)
- Competitive value
  —Standardization of materials and processes

  —Supply chain management

  —Inventory management

  —JIT II/administrative reduction

  —Pooling agreements
- Customer satisfaction
  —Responsiveness (administrative and technical support)

  —On-time delivery (product, tooling, data)

  —Technology sharing/partnering

  —Next operation as customers

  —Employee deployment

  —Continued process improvement activities

On a regular basis, suppliers are requested to submit their continuous improvement plans for each of the four areas. Process mapping of the supplier's processes is done to discover which processes the company's products flow through. Suppliers are asked what assistance they require and what the expected mutual gains are from the assistance.

In order to better measure supplier performance capabilities, the company has developed a corporate supplier survey that involves training auditors in conducting supplier quality surveys. The survey instrument has a structure based on Malcolm Baldrige National Quality Award criteria (management systems, quality information, subsupplier control, customer satisfaction, process planning and control, and new product development). All of the company's major suppliers are going through this audit process, and the information is being put onto a corporation-wide database.

Ramp-up and Timing Capabilities. It is no longer enough for a supplier to be able to design and manufacture a prototype or start up small volume production. Because of the intense competition and short product life cycles in many industries (such as electronics and computers), suppliers must also be able to meet product introduction deadlines and ramp-up their production volumes very quickly. Several of the companies we studied assessed these criteria through a variety of means.

CASE EXAMPLE

Upside Flexibility

For one computer manufacturer, the supplier's capacity and flexibility are critical issues, and the team will examine what kind of agreements the supplier has with its contract manufacturers and how they affect the supplier's ability to increase output quickly. The supplier must have upside flexibility requirements amounting to

- 25 percent up in 4 weeks
- 50 percent up in 8 weeks
- 100 percent up in 12 weeks

CASE EXAMPLE

Know Your Suppliers

A computer peripherals manufacturer faces the problem of having a very limited number of potential suppliers of several of its key components, worldwide. However, because of the small number of suppliers, the company has done business with most of them and has experience with their capabilities. Supplier selection is based primarily on the supplier's capability to design and manufacture the product in large volumes to performance specifications within the required time.

Innovation and Technical Assessment. Several of the companies carried out detailed assessments of the suppliers' technical capabilities prior to selecting them for a new product development project. In most cases, both formal and informal approaches were required to develop a reliable assessment. A typical approach would start with a formal standard survey-type assessment, which would be augmented by informal assessments by internal engineer's assessments based on face-to-face discussions with the supplier's technical personnel. The most detailed technical assessments considered both of these inputs, as informal discussions can often reveal problems that may not be obvious to an external uninformed party.

CASE EXAMPLE

Total Cost Assessment

Suppliers involved early in one chemical company's development efforts are evaluated using a number of criteria in a total cost of ownership type of model that considers

- Reputation for meeting requirements
- Cost/availability of raw materials
- Difficulty of the process matched against the supplier's capability
- Waste generated in the supplier's process

(continued)

- Number of steps required of the supplier
- Environmental compliance
- Technical competence

The choice of supplier is a decision made by the whole team, but not everyone on the team necessarily gets directly involved. A smaller group within the commercialization team may make a recommendation. Following the recommendation, the company audits the supplier's facilities for contamination, environmental compliance, technical capability, cost, quality, and location, which are all weighted (weights vary by commodity).

CASE EXAMPLE

Self-Assessment Survey

At one computer company, in the first stage of the new product development process (definition and planning), material support involves selection of a technology given the requirements of the product. Once this is complete, the corporate materials group can come up with a potential list of suppliers. If the supplier is new to the company, the supplier will first perform a self-assessment survey. Then the team will visit for several days and examine eight separate modules, including quality systems, control, reliability, and financial analysis, and arrive at a performance score.

CASE EXAMPLE

Rely on Other Customers' Judgment

An automotive company is seeking to certify full-service suppliers using cross-functional teams. Full on-site technical surveys are conducted. The cross-functional team verifies the supplier's self-assessment. Issues include hardware, software, technology, facilities, and so on. With critical suppliers, the team may evaluate the supplier's capability and then come back and develop the product around the supplier's capabilities. The company is already very familiar with some suppliers, so there is little beyond the self-assessment. In cases when the company is a relatively small customer, it will rely on the fact that other larger world-class customers use the supplier and that a self-assessment also suffices.

Training. Training/development is another key consideration when integrating suppliers into new product development efforts. Supplier capabilities are dependent on key skills of personnel throughout the organization. Training audits can serve as one means for ensuring high quality personnel exist to support supplier performance.

CASE EXAMPLE

Training Audits

One of the companies studied has a detailed evaluation of the background and training of the supplier's personnel being used to start a new process within the company's facility. Every supplier technician is audited. There is a major shortage of qualified technicians (in fact, the company has gotten into the habit of placing major want-ads in areas where there have been significant military layoffs). For this reason, technician audits are deemed critical to ensure that the process stays up and running, continually generating revenues.

Initially, a phase 1 audit has the person filling out a form. Ninety to 95 percent of applicants make it through this phase. The auditors include purchasing, engineering, manufacturing supervisor, and so on, who put together profile expectations and review the technicians' skills vis-à-vis these expectations. The end objective of a phase 1 audit is to identify potential technicians for phase 2 audits.

A phase 2 audit is a personal review of the personnel. Only 5 to 10 percent of the technicians are required to go through this type of audit. The individual must be able to interact with the internal team, and there are also cultural issues with regard to how well he or she works with the organization. Questions include behavioral questions (customer service interaction), technical questions (asked by engineers, regarding maintenance and so on), and cultural questions (such as whether he or she agrees with the company's tenets).

If an individual fails a phase 2 audit, he or she goes through additional training, or provides back-up to other more highly trained technicians until further training takes place. Most of the 10 percent of all technicians who go through phase 2 make it. Finally, a phase 3 audit maps out the exact maintenance tasks and the relative level of the technician before start-up. Any discrepancies are resolved before production begins. The company closely monitors the scheduled date for start-up, including the number of people showing up on schedule.

Building Relationships

In addition to selecting the right suppliers to start with, another part of building an effective supply base is developing the right relationships with the suppliers. As companies integrate suppliers into new product development efforts, they find themselves having to work much more closely and cooperatively with those suppliers than ever before. Building appropriate, solid relationships is critical.

CASE EXAMPLE

Five Times the Effort

At one computer manufacturer we studied, design engineers work closely with supplier engineers during product design. About 10 percent of the time, a design team must integrate a new supplier to obtain breakthrough technology. Managers estimate that about five times the effort is required to bring on a new supplier compared to an existing supplier.

Several of the companies we studied have established strategic alliances with the suppliers they are integrating into the earliest stages of new product development. These relationships are based on common strategic interests of the companies and provide a foundation for close, cooperative work between the organizations.

Step 4a—Summary

Prior to integrating a supplier into a new product development initiative, detailed supplier capability and performance assessment should be carried out. It should assess major performance criteria related to the supplier's technology, cost, price, quality, and ramp-up capability. This assessment should be systematically carried out based on both hard performance data and subjective assessments by technical personnel. Performance data should be weighted in such a manner that they are aligned with customer performance requirements. The output of this assessment should provide an overall picture of the supplier's potential for development and manufacture of the required component/subsystem.

STEP 5A—ALIGN OBJECTIVES AND TECHNOLOGY ROAD MAPS

Even after a detailed performance assessment has been carried out prior to selection, there is a second type of assessment that must be carried out and an associated ongoing management task. These have to do with ensuring the alignment, both long-term and short-term, of the objectives and the technology plans of the buying company and the supplier.

To obtain maximum strategic benefit from the integration of the supplier, the companies should have shared objectives and complementary future technology plans. This is most commonly described in terms of a convergence of the companies' technology road maps, which describe the performance, cost, and technology characteristics of future products each company plans to develop/introduce over some specified time period.

The specific approaches companies use to assess and achieve alignment of technology road maps with suppliers vary considerably. Regardless of the specific approach, sharing information is one critical element of the process. A second important element is providing some incentive or motivation for suppliers to work at alignment with the buying company.

Sharing Technology Road Map Information

Sharing technology road map information between the buying company and suppliers (or potential suppliers) is an important tool for achieving alignment. To the extent that each company has visibility of the other's technology plans, both have the opportunity to see where their plans align and, perhaps, where their plans diverge. If there is divergence, either company or both companies may alter their plans to create better alignment.

CASE EXAMPLE

It Started with a Hunch

At one company, one of the best supplier integration examples was a relationship that was initiated by an engineer in the buying company. The engineer thought he saw synergies in the capabilities of his company and a supplier and began talking informally with a counterpart in the supplier company. This led to a high-level meeting between executives from the two companies. At this meeting, supplier executives shared technology plans and road maps and identified common research streams in a very broad category of materials. An executive consensus was reached regarding what the buying company wanted to work on next to support the next product or product family. A list of the top four projects was targeted directly to future product needs, both short-term and long-term. This relationship has now become institutionalized, with the two companies meeting periodically to share their road maps and update the project list.

CASE EXAMPLE

Establish Trust Upfront

One computer company shares technology road maps with specific suppliers, based on nondisclosure agreements that are part of a broad general agreement with the supplier. Suppliers also share their technology road maps. Both parties may change their designs based on future road map directions. A chip supplier may include specific features for unique customers, in what may become a future standard chip design. Only trusted suppliers who currently supply significant volumes are provided with general information on future products.

CASE EXAMPLE

Alliances Only

Some companies develop special relationships with suppliers in order to facilitate the sharing of information and the alignment of plans and objectives. One company we studied integrates only suppliers that have been formally accepted as strategic alliance partners.

The company defines a strategic alliance business relationship as one in which "participants willingly invest in changing their fundamental business practices for purposes of reducing duplication and waste and facilitating improved performance." Firms have "joint ownership in the relationship, equally share in benefits achieved and recognize equal risks in managing the relationship." The basic characteristics of the relationship are

- Interdependent arrangement between the company and the supplier to increasingly integrate aspects of their businesses in order to improve quality, responsiveness, cost, asset investment, and time-to-market

- Long-term

- Limited to a small group of suppliers (typically fewer than 20) who provide products, services, or technical expertise that is pivotal toward the supplier's and the customer's reaching their respective and joint business goals

- Willingness of both parties to invest in the human resources and the identified financial resources needed to support a long-term business relationship

(continued)

- Frequent and meaningful two-sided performance feedback (structured and unstructured) between both parties: performance reviews that focus on measuring and tracking operational performance in the context of overall strategic direction and harmony, and communications that help build personal relationships between the parties

- Empowerment of primary contact employees by senior management to make decisions to maintain and improve operational performance as well as cost competitiveness and supply integration

- A trusting relationship between the firms, which focuses on

  1. Developing trust throughout both companies

  2. Creating loyalty toward the long-term success of the relationship

  3. Building strong commitment to the process

  4. Heightening overall responsiveness to joint operational and market needs

  5. Developing a continuous improvement mindset about the total supply chain

- Complementary cultures

- Willingness of both parties to abandon traditional business practices and operational methodologies to optimize the total supply chain

- Relationship structured to begin on a relatively small scale in order to allow for growth and development of personal relationships

- Specific steps that describe how the alliance can be dissolved to minimize the negative effect on both firms; rules and impartial avenues at both ends to open discussions about eroding behaviors and remedies

To make this kind of relationship successful in the long term, the company has identified several mandatory requirements:

- A special system or process to resolve difficult matters and address controversial issues is created and supported by both parties. Senior management is kept informed of these matters.

- A resource catalog showing human and nonhuman resources provided by each party is kept current and resides at both businesses. The catalog identifies the resource, the cost of the item, the approximate time it was contributed to the accord, the names and titles of senior management who are aware of the item(s), and the party providing each.

- An up-to-date description of the business direction and long-term strategy is shared between the firms.

- A current set of organizational charts and responsibilities is shared between the firms.

- A system of review and evaluation to help dissolve a strategic alliance relationship exists.

- A written accord states that the customer will target purchasing opportunities toward the supplier's offerings in all areas of strategic significance. The areas of strategic significance relate to the products/services being provided to the customer by the supplier. The customer will join with the supplier in continually identifying new areas where the supplier can expand product or service in a way that does not conflict with other allies.

- A written accord states that the supplier in the alliance will provide the lowest total cost of ownership to the customer in all areas of strategic significance. The supplier will join with the customer in continually identifying ways to improve the cost competitiveness of the offering. Both parties will invest resources to support the process and will share in the financial and operational benefits of the cost improvements based on their share of the resources applied.

CASE EXAMPLE

Hitting the "Sweet Spot"

A different type of road map sharing is done by one electronics company whose managers are unsure where needed technology developments are most likely to occur. In select cases, internal development groups will share early information about future technology road maps with just about any global supplier who will listen in an attempt to ensure that the required technology will eventually be available. For instance, in one commodity, the manager has established a technology map with performance curves, and expected targets by date. The target area is essentially the "sweet spot," which is shown to suppliers. Suppliers are told that if they can't hit the sweet spot by the target date, they won't get the business. This concept is somewhat different than conventional early involvement. Because of the volatility of this industry, the company does not have the time or the need to form alliances and go through an early involvement program. Rather, the strategy is to make sure the technology is available by openly sharing technology road maps with any qualified supplier who will listen and moving business around to take advantage of performance at the target price.

Within the computer industry, many companies are pushing for greater standardization of components. In this industry, a number of manufacturers, customers, and suppliers meet on a quarterly basis to discuss emerging standards. This industry collaboration is beneficial for all players involved. Manufacturers may better manage new product introductions as the standards help them plan their product designs. Suppliers are able to identify technology requirements early, which allows them to invest in the capabilities and capacity requirements needed to meet challenging project goals. Further, suppliers may influence or develop standards that are relevant to their products and processes.

Motivating Supplier Alignment

In addition to sharing the information needed to understand the degree of alignment that exists between the buying company and its supplier, there must be some means of encouraging the supplier to work toward greater alignment. In most cases, the prospect of future business with the buying company is enough. In other situations, there may be other motivations for the supplier to work at alignment with the buying company.

CASE EXAMPLE

Image Is Everything

One auto company we studied was able to secure supplier commitments for one of its new product development projects with little or no guaranteed profit opportunity. The desire of suppliers to be involved with this project was based on the potential image benefit— the suppliers hoped that being involved in and performing well in an innovative project utilizing new technologies would build their visibility and reputation. Some suppliers also viewed the project as a means of establishing a business relationship with the company and getting their foot in the door. The company's supplier strategy has changed supplier behavior from a low-quote mentality to a long-term development culture. The overall shift may take several years to occur, and part of the barriers to overcome are internal.

CASE EXAMPLE

Low-Volume Supplier

An electronics company we studied has developed a very good relationship with one of its suppliers, in which they worked jointly on development of new materials. Each company brings some expertise to the process which the other company lacks. There is no real incentive for the supplier in terms of substantial future business with this buying company; the volumes involved are simply too small. As a part of the agreement, however, the supplier may use the new technologies and materials developed to market noncompeting products to other customers.

SUMMARY

The selection and alignment of suppliers for integration into new product development is clearly a major part of the process. The end result of these two steps is a world-class supply base whose goals and objectives are aligned with those of the buying company. The buying company and its suppliers must have developed a well-defined map for future technologies and specified criteria for measurement and development of the relationship. Despite this planning effort, however, the buying company must be aware of changes in technologies that might provoke changes in the supply strategy. This is particularly important in dynamic industries where technologies are changing dramatically and affect competitiveness. For this reason, companies must also constantly maintain a vigil on emerging technologies and align their future supply strategies with potential changes in technologies. This series of steps is described in the next chapter.

Chapter 6

Establishing a Bookshelf of Viable Technologies and Suppliers

"The challenge is to scan the horizon to identify new and emerging technologies, assess their risk, and 'bookshelf' them. Once we have the technology 'on the bookshelf,' we can pull it down, and wheel it in just in time to meet the product release deadline."

Emerging technologies product manager

INTRODUCTION

Technology is a critical issue in new product development (see Figure 6.1). Advances in product or process technology can provide significant competitive advantage, and being first to market with a new technology can result in a substantial market share advantage. New technology, however, can be a double-edged sword. Development of new technologies often requires huge investment, and if the technology doesn't pan out, in addition to the wasted investment, product launch may be delayed and product cost or performance targets may not be met.

Technological uncertainty/risk comes from several sources:

- "New to the world" technologies
- New applications of existing technologies
- Technologies outside the company's field of expertise

The newer a technology, the greater the risk associated with applying that technology in a new product (see Figure 6.2). If a technology is new to the company, but not new to the world, the company can mitigate the risk by working with a supplier that has significant experience with the technology. Longer term, if the technology is critical to the buying company's product, the company may want to develop internal capability with the technology.

Many companies are facing an increase in technological risk/uncertainty due to their desire to reduce product development cycle times while at the same time maintaining their level of innovativeness. In this situation, organizations find themselves having to commit to technology and design decisions earlier, and often with less information. However, technological risk in new product development can be managed. With careful planning and

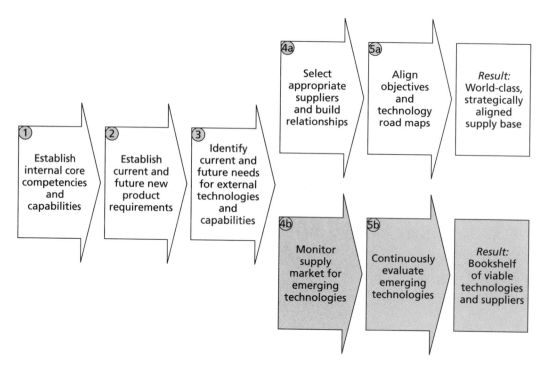

Figure 6.1. Supplier integration strategic planning process.

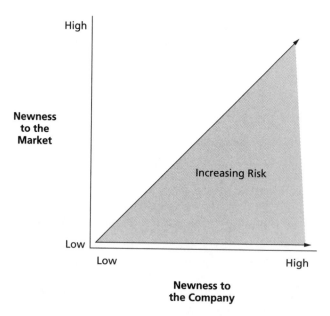

Figure 6.2. Relative technological risk.

decision making, a firm can control its exposure to technological risk and still realize the benefits of technological advances. Monitoring the market for emerging technologies and continuously evaluating those technologies for applicability in new products are steps critical to managing this risk.

STEP 4B—MONITOR SUPPLY MARKET FOR EMERGING TECHNOLOGIES

In this process step, the organization must continuously monitor possible emerging technologies. Many of the different techniques for doing so were described in chapter 5.

CASE EXAMPLE

Sharing Road Maps

In one company studied, the sharing of technology road maps often strongly influenced the type of buyer/supplier interactions that resulted in the new product development process. The actual process of sharing information occurred in a variety of forms, which in some cases influenced the type of relationship that emerged:

- Two-way information sharing between buyer and seller
- One-way sharing (buyer to many suppliers)
- Supplier councils tied to new product development
- Technology fairs

This Japanese company has formed an industry group where customers, manufacturers, and suppliers meet every quarter to review proposals and share opinions on emerging product standards. Over 250 companies are involved in the effort. Two acceptable standards have been adopted largely through these efforts.

In sharing road maps, it must be recognized that supplier involvement in new product development can have effects, both positive and negative, on technology risk/uncertainty. Positive effects include the following:

- The supplier may have greater experience or expertise with the technology and, as a result, may have better information about where the technology can be successfully applied.
- Some (or all) of the technological risk may be taken on by the supplier.
- The buying firm may have some ability to influence the direction of the supplier's research and development efforts in order to match developing technologies with the buying firm's technology strategy.
- If a closer relationship between the buying company and the supplier develops as a result of supplier involvement, the supplier may be more willing to share information about its new/emerging technologies with the buying company.

Negative effects may be these:

- Involvement with a supplier may lock the buying company in to the supplier and its technologies. This makes initial selection of the supplier a more critical issue, as the buying company needs to anticipate whether the supplier will remain a technology leader.

- A supplier with inside track may not have as much incentive to innovate, slowing the pace of technological advancement. The buying company must find a way to make sure it is getting the supplier's best efforts.

CASE EXAMPLE

Advanced Technology Groups

One of the companies we studied, which uses supplier-provided technologies extensively in its new products, has established an advanced technology group charged with managing the development and adoption of new technologies for the company's products. The group monitors the supply market for new technologies and also takes a proactive role in developing technologies called for by the company's product line teams. In some cases, the advanced technology group will undertake development itself, and in other cases, it will pursue suppliers to develop the technology.

This company has also implemented what it calls a "window of technology" process to help improve its access to new or developing technologies. The process, managed by the advanced technology group, provides a single point of contact in the company for a supplier who wants to propose a new technology or new product idea to the company. The supplier's idea gets a fair hearing, but the information is handled confidentially by the advanced technology group, so the idea is protected. If the company is interested in the idea, it may commit to specific volume with the supplier or may work with the supplier to develop the technology further.

In order to prevent a situation in which a buying company is shut out of a given technology and misses a market opportunity, the company must continuously evaluate these emerging technologies.

STEP 5B—CONTINUOUSLY EVALUATE EMERGING TECHNOLOGIES

In evaluating a given technology, the buying company must perform a risk assessment, which essentially measures the probability of successfully applying the technology in a new product/process/service. This requires a judgment on the degree of robustness of the technology as well as the potential for future integration. A number of strategies might be used to evaluate and control or manage technological uncertainty/risk in new product development:

- Screens or hurdles may be established in the NPD process where a "go or no-go" decision will be made on the application of a particular technology. At some stage, if the viability or readiness of the technology is not certain, it is dropped from the application. The earlier this type of hurdle is placed in the NPD process, the less risk is incurred.

- A company may have different tolerance for risk in different application settings, depending on the implications of a technology problem or failure in that application. Where consequences of failure are severe, the company will have less tolerance for risk than where consequences are relatively minor.

- A company may share its technology road maps with its suppliers (and vice versa). This strategy has several potential benefits:

  —The buying company can find out early if its technology plans will not be supported by its suppliers' planned developments.

  —The buying company may be able to influence suppliers to work on the technologies that will be of greatest value to the buying company.

  —The buying company may be able to alter its own technology road map to be better aligned with what its suppliers will be working on.

  —The buying company may try to get its technological requirements built into industry-standard components.

An important issue for companies that want to apply new technologies in their new products is how to time the introduction of the technology. If they try to apply the technology too soon, it may fail. On the other hand, if they wait too long, they may lose the competitive advantage of being first in the market with the innovation. (see Figure 6.3).

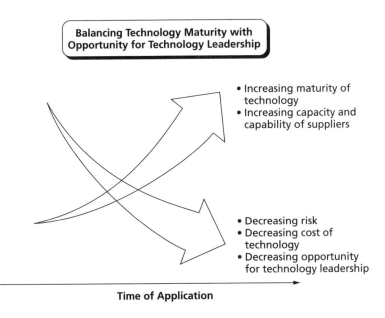

Figure 6.3. Technology leadership opportunity.

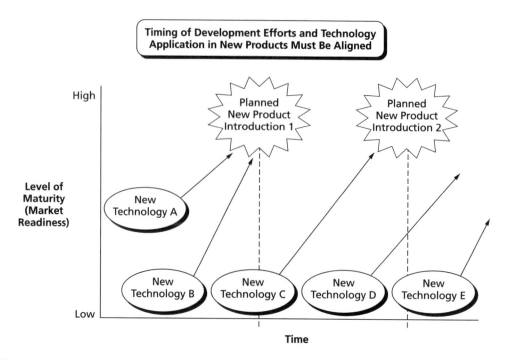

Figure 6.4. Managing product and technology development.

For example, in the computer industry, a key challenge lies in the timing of application of new technology. In some cases, a supplier can provide a promising new technology that is not yet robust and not cost competitive. Over time, this situation may change, as costs are lowered and technological performance also improves. Thus, a decision must be made about when to transition a new technology into the product cycle. This can be very difficult, since the technology may be untested or substandard, yet other producers are already using it. On the downside, if it is not incorporated, they run the risk of being late to market with a new feature or technology. In this industry, new products come out on the average of every six months.

From a strategic perspective, what companies facing this issue would like to do is to manage new technology development and application so that they are synchronized (see Figure 6.4). In effect, this is equivalent to placing a technology that is premature on a bookshelf, and taking it off the bookshelf for application when it is sufficiently robust, cost-effective, or practical to apply.

Technology uncertainty is not inherently bad; it is a fact of life for any company operating in an industry where technology is evolving. The key for these companies is to understand the level of uncertainty they face with any given technology and to understand how much risk they are willing to tolerate. Typically, their tolerance for uncertainty or risk will vary depending on how near they are to trying to bring the technology to market in a specific product application (see Figure 6.5).

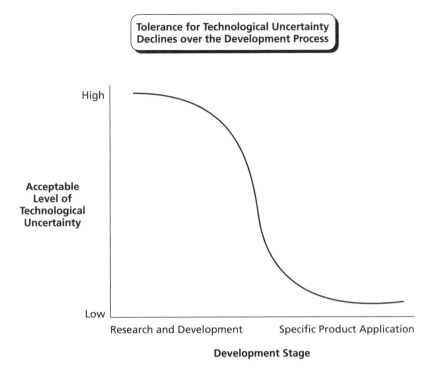

Figure 6.5. Technology uncertainty tolerance.

CASE EXAMPLE

Shift the Tolerance-for-Risk Curve

One of the companies we studied is in the process of trying to significantly accelerate its rate of new product development. One way the company is attempting to do this is by increasing its willingness to take a risk by moving into the commercialization stage earlier in the development process, with less information. The company has explicitly shifted its risk-tolerance curve.

Strategies are available to help ensure that promising new technologies get developed and new developments get a fair hearing:

- Some buying companies have established advanced technology groups as a part of their procurement organization. The role of the advanced technology group is to monitor the market for new/developing technologies that may have applications to the buying company's products and to make sure that the buying company has access to those technologies when it needs them.

- Sharing technology road maps with suppliers can also help the buying company ensure that the right technologies are being developed at the right time.

In the following company examples, we provide specific illustrations of how companies approach this issue of managing technology risk and the timing of technology application.

A Make or Break Issue

One automotive company believes that technology uncertainty is a make or break issue in product development. The company will not proceed with plans to use a new technology in a new product application unless it is certain the new technology will work and will be available on time. The company likes to own the new technology because this gives it greater control over the development.

Technology Test Beds

Another automotive company has used a low-volume product line as a type of test bed for new technology applications. Exposure is limited because of the lower volume, but the company uses the product line as a showcase as well, so suppliers are willing to work with the company on the application of the new technologies.

Commonize Parts

An electronics company has made a major effort to get its designers to commonize parts across products. This helps to increase the company's level of certainty regarding the technologies and designs being used in the new products.

Involve the Second Tier

One company has found that second-tier raw material suppliers are often the technology leaders in its industry, rather than the first-tier suppliers who process the raw material. Thus, the company is trying to get raw material suppliers involved in its development process. Often, to achieve this involvement, the company must make early commitment of its business. This is a risky proposition because some of the technologies are changing rapidly.

Connect the Dots

One of the companies we studied uses a coding system to describe the maturity level of various technologies it is using or considering. Each is designated as a green, amber, or red dot technology:

- Green dots: well-known technologies that are internally developed and perfected

- Amber dots: not well known

- Red dots: new technology (high failure rates)

The company avoids using red dot technologies in new products and tries to minimize the use of amber dot technologies.

SUMMARY

In seeking to identify and evaluate technologies for risk, the following guidelines emerged:

- Limit exposure to technological risk.

    —Implement screens in the new product development process to force careful examination of the viability of a technology application before the process proceeds too far.

    —Limit the number of new technologies being used in any one new product development effort.

    —Leverage technologies already available and with which the company already has significant experience.

- Manage technological risk strategically.

    —Understand which technologies have the potential to have an impact on product performance as perceived by the customer. Focus consideration of new or riskier technologies on those that will impress the customer.

    —Try out less-mature technologies in markets where the impact of technology problems is less severe.

- Try to manage future technology development proactively.

    —Maintain technology road maps and share them with key suppliers to help ensure alignment of current development efforts (both internal and external) with future technology needs.

    —Work with key suppliers to build needed features or capabilities into industry-standard components.

    —Establish an advance technology group in the organization to actively monitor new technology developments and to ensure that proposals from developers of new technologies receive a fair hearing.

    —Bookshelf new technologies so they will be mature and available for future applications.

Chapter 7

Determining the Supplier's Role and Setting Targets

"Establishing targets is both a top-down and a bottom-up process."

Supply manager at automotive company

INTRODUCTION

A world-class strategically aligned supply base, coupled with a bookshelf of viable technologies, enables the supplier integration execution process. The purpose of the execution process is to ensure that each party maximizes the value of the combined knowledge and capabilities in order to meet or exceed customer requirements. Key issues in the execution process focus on enhancing the quality of the supplier's participation in the design process. The supplier integration execution process model is illustrated in Figure 7.1.

- Step 1, give supplier(s) an active role on the project team, is intended to identify roles and responsibilities and to drive both buyer and supplier ownership of the NPD effort. This step precedes specific design and development activities. Key points of contact and decision makers are identified, and the infrastructure to support communication and participation is developed and/or refined.

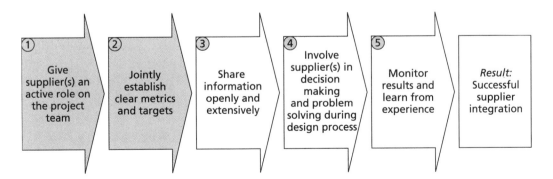

Figure 7.1. Supplier integration execution process.

137

- Step 2, jointly establish clear metrics and targets, further drives ownership in the NPD process and formally defines the expectations and responsibilities of all involved parties. This step also guides the development effort by providing a system for measuring progress and tracking.

- Step 3, share information openly and extensively, is critical for NPD success. The open, honest, and timely communication of business and technical data ensures that goals are still aligned and requirements and specifications understood, and facilitates better decision making and problem resolution at earlier stages in the NPD effort.

- Step 4, involve supplier(s) in decision making and problem solving during the design process, focuses on specific design and development activities. To maximize the combined capabilities of both organizations, it is necessary to allow suppliers to provide input to decisions that should be jointly made and to give them the freedom to make decisions in areas where they are the expert.

- Step 5, monitor results and learn from experience, calls for performance measurement throughout the development process and volume production. Properly implemented, the performance measures can be used for feedback to correct the current development effort, as well as to make strategic and tactical adjustments to future development efforts.

Each of the execution process steps is discussed in detail in the following sections. Before proceeding, however, it is worth repeating two key points:

1. The strategic planning process lays the foundation for the execution process. By developing a world-class strategically aligned supply base, the buying firm has proactively identified the suppliers that have the skills, technologies, business acumen, and ethical conduct required for successful supplier integration. Also, by developing a bookshelf of viable technologies, the buying firm has aligned its technical and business goals with that of its key suppliers. Further, throughout the strategic planning phase, lines of communication are established, trust is built, and a sense of teaming is developed prior to a specific development effort.

2. Although the execution process model is depicted as a sequential process, this is not strictly the case. For example, information sharing (shown as step 3) is critical throughout both the strategic planning and execution processes. Further, similar strategies and processes are used to give suppliers an active role on the project team (step 1) and to involve suppliers in decision making and problem solving during the design process (step 4). Clearly, the execution process consists of interdependent activities that must be flexibly managed to achieve optimal results.

GIVE SUPPLIER(S) AN ACTIVE ROLE ON THE PROJECT TEAM

Buying companies that make suppliers active participants on the NPD project team achieve higher levels of supplier integration success than those companies that limit suppliers' participation. This does not mean that all suppliers should actively participate in the everyday activities of the project team. Rather, suppliers should participate as a member of the project team at a level commensurate with their expected contribution. The higher the complexity and criticality of the supplied item, the greater the level of supplier participation on the core project team. With less complex but nonetheless critical items, supplier participation may be more appropriate at the support team level or at a lower level core team.

Giving suppliers an active role prior to specific design and development is intended to ensure each party clearly understands what is expected of it during NPD, and to develop a sense of ownership and team commitment. Most firms studied in this project use a team approach for developing new products. Related research conducted at Michigan State University revealed that more than 80 percent of firms surveyed plan to use teams to support some part of their sourcing effort, including new product development.[1] Earlier research also identified a link between supplier participation on cross-functional teams and positive performance outcomes. Actively including suppliers as part of the product or project team can be a differentiating success factor.

When executed properly, teams should expect formal supplier participation to enhance integration efforts while positively affecting team performance. Even teams where suppliers are informal rather than formal participants should realize certain positive outcomes. Teams that successfully promote supplier participation at team meetings (either as formal members or informal participants) should expect:

- Higher assessments of team effort from observers external to the buying company

- Greater quality of information exchange between the team and its key suppliers

- Fewer problems coordinating work activity between the team and its key suppliers

- Greater performance improvement support from suppliers compared with teams that do not involve suppliers

Various approaches support the integration of suppliers into the NPD process. Without some or all of these in place, interfirm coordination and collaboration becomes difficult or nonexistent. Specific approaches frequently identified in the field research include:

- Directly extending the strategic planning process

- Establishing top management support at the buyer and supplier early in the process

- Maintaining a project/finished product focus versus functional focus

- Reaching cross-functional team consensus regarding the choice of suppliers

- Formally defining roles and responsibilities of buyer and supplier

- Creating buyer-supplier team permanency/stability

- Using contractual mechanisms to encourage supplier commitment

- Defining ownership of new product/process technology

---

[1]Monczka, Robert M. and Robert J. Trent, "Cross-Functional Sourcing Team Effectiveness," a study published by the Center for Advanced Purchasing Studies, Tempe, Arizona (1993).

Directly Extending the Strategic Planning Process

As a natural extension of the strategic planning process, many companies attempt to either review or strengthen their relationships prior to actual design execution to gain supplier commitment and involvement in the NPD effort.

CASE EXAMPLE

Visit Suppliers

A leading Japanese firm visits its key suppliers before the detailed design of a new product begins. The company uses established supplier relationships to support identification of suppliers to include on product development teams. These visits help the purchaser decide if the supplier can produce an item at the targeted cost and quality levels. The buyer also assesses the supplier's ability to become part of the product development team. After a general discussion about the item required to support the new product, the supplier submits an initial design proposal. As the development cycle progresses, the design becomes progressively tighter and detailed. Starting with a basic frame and shape based only on broad product requirements, the product design evolves, with engineers from both companies working together to evaluate alternative designs that satisfy product requirements.

CASE EXAMPLE

Multiple Projects

A second company, a global electronics firm, creates joint supplier/buyer teams to work on four technology or product development projects simultaneously. Each firm assigns personnel to the teams, with commitment to this approach detailed in a formal partnership agreement. Depending on the project, team involvement has evolved to the point where the supplier sometimes takes a lead role and ownership for the project's outcome. The supplier shares risks and rewards with the buyer and accepts accountability for performance outcomes.

CASE EXAMPLE

Supplier Development Manager

Another leading firm has created the position of supply chain development manager. This position has the authority to include key suppliers during new product development, either as formal team members or as informal participants. Supplier integration is evolving to the point where supplier-to-supplier interaction is occurring as supply chain development managers initiate ways to further improve product and process development. Suppliers are now becoming part of product design teams at corporate headquarters.

Resolve Culture Gaps

One firm suggested that corporate cultural differences are an issue when including suppliers on design and development teams. This firm, which relies heavily on supplier support during the development of process equipment, includes supplier representatives as part of its process design teams. It has found it challenging to deal with the different corporate cultures that exist across its supply base. During one project, a major supplier assumed a lead role for developing a process for use by all of the buying company's suppliers. The project required suppliers with different corporate and national cultures, some of whom were also competitors, to work together. Getting these suppliers to collaborate became a major challenge for the lead supplier.

Establishing Top Management Support at the Buyer and Supplier Organizations Early in the Process

The changes required to support integrative product and process development will require, over the longer term, executive commitment at buying and supplying firms. Integration usually requires a commitment of personnel, budget, and time to craft agreements conveying the willingness of parties to work together. By providing the resources required to pursue supplier integration, executive management also sends a visible message that integration is a strategic pursuit that can help create competitive advantage.

Executive commitment does not mean that executive management becomes involved in the day-to-day activities of the development effort. Instead, commitment usually signifies that executive management endorses early involvement objectives and agrees to support the needs of that involvement. Furthermore, executive commitment often involves higher-level interaction between firms with the purpose of identifying future joint involvement opportunities.

Executive Commitment

At one firm noted for its progressive use of early involvement, executive management, along with management from a carefully selected supplier, sponsored a higher-level committee to investigate the feasibility of pursuing joint longer-term technology development projects. Once the committee reported on the feasibility of pursuing projects jointly, executive management at both firms signed a two-page memorandum signifying their support of joint involvement efforts. This memorandum also outlined each party's commitment of resources required to support joint development projects. Technology development projects now occur before formal product or process development. Joint technology development teams are responsible for developing a new technology and then transferring that technology to an integrated product and process

(continued)

development team for commercialization. While both firms endorse joint development efforts, executive management allows the execution of the process to be the responsibility of lower-level staff.

Steering Committee

At a second company, a new chief purchasing officer created a structure that pursues continuous early involvement as a strategic objective. Before formulating a procurement and sourcing vision, this firm's vice president of supply visited each business unit to determine the status of the supply function. He then established a cross-organizational steering committee of supply executives and charged it with identifying areas of competency essential to success. One area identified as critical to success was increased supplier integration. To support this firm's strategic effort, the vice president of supply created several highly visible executive-level positions responsible for supporting and executing companywide the supply management strategic plan. This plan forwards the company's objectives in the areas identified as essential to success, including supplier integration. The company evaluates supplier involvement during product and process development at each business unit and quantifies how this helped to reduce costs, cycle times, and defect rates and improve product reliability.

Coaching Executive

While executive support is critical, a risk is present when executive management is uninformed or does not understand early supplier involvement. According to one firm, the involvement process is simplified if executive management is "coachable" and receptive to involving suppliers early in product and process development. However, if executive management perceives that early involvement presents too many risks or becomes too involved in the execution of the process, early involvement efforts may not be as successful. Representatives from this firm argue that commitment must come from executive management, but execution should remain the responsibility of those closest to the process.

Get Them Interested

Initial demonstrations of executive commitment to early involvement may also come from suppliers rather than the buying company. For example, an innovative new product development project that received widespread industry attention attracted the interest of certain suppliers. These suppliers showed their commitment to this project and to early involvement by building and colocating in a new facility near the buying firm. Furthermore, several suppliers assumed responsibility for program management by coordinating the development of product subassemblies.

Maintaining a Project/Finished Product Focus versus Functional Focus

Maintaining a functional rather than product or combined product/functional focus compounds the challenges associated with integrating suppliers into new product and process development. Most firms studied during the field research phase of this project maintained full-time product development teams or managed a matrix organizational structure. With the matrix structure, team members divide time between the product/process development team and regular job responsibilities. Most firms are attempting to move away from a strictly functional focus, particularly as it relates to new product development. Procurement is increasingly supporting a finished product versus functional focus, primarily by participating on new product/process development teams and closer interaction with engineering groups.

Within sourcing, most firms will argue the need to maintain some level of commodity expertise. However, even commodity expertise is becoming cross-functional rather than functional. Also, product and process development often requires participation from product/process development teams and commodity teams. The commodity teams support product development teams by providing current information about the items and sources considered during product development. The sourcing representative on the product/process team maintains a product/process focus while commodity team members take a broader perspective. At one firm, it is the responsibility of the product development team's sourcing member to coordinate sourcing requirements with the correct commodity team.

CASE EXAMPLE

Standardize Across Projects

Companies maintain a commodity and finished product focus in a variety of ways. At one firm, a commodity focus within purchasing/supply helps promote standardization across product development projects. Furthermore, a commodity focus also supports cost comparisons across projects or items. These comparisons might not be possible if the product development team was singularly responsible for identifying and sourcing single items or subassemblies. When developing new products, this firm relies on full-time platform teams with commodity team participation.

CASE EXAMPLE

Don't Overcustomize

One company requires that commodity team representatives meet with product development teams to ensure the teams do not overcustomize the final product design. This firm, which is under intense pressure to reduce product cost, makes sure that development

(continued)

teams consider, whenever possible, the use of building blocks during design. Building blocks are off-the-shelf or previously designed components or subassemblies that, when used in a new design, may help reduce product cost by reusing established designs. Using building blocks can also promote product simplification and consistent performance. Design teams cannot finalize a product's design without first determining if appropriate/usable building blocks exist.

Globalized Technologies

Increased globalization of the sourcing process has created additional challenges when coordinating design and development efforts. For example, one firm organizes around design and product centers of excellence. Product development may occur at a different geographical center than the center responsible for sourcing a commodity item required by the team. Within this environment, coordination mechanisms, such as information technology, become critical.

A project/finished product focus will better support early supplier involvement efforts. A shift has occurred over the last few years away from a strict purchasing functional focus toward one that is better able to support the needs of product development teams. Furthermore, many firms will still maintain their commodity expertise by creating commodity teams that interact with and support product development teams.

Reaching Cross-Functional Team Consensus
Regarding the Choice of Supplier(s)

Supplier choice has several dimensions. The first, which is also the broadest, involves selecting suppliers to provide material during the development and eventual production of a new product. The second, which is more complex, involves agreement about the suppliers who are capable and willing to be early participants during product and process development.

Increasingly, supplier selection during new product and process development is becoming a team rather than a functional/individual responsibility. Often, purchasing assumes an informational or advisory role with new product development teams during selection. The emphasis on team-based product development can cause the source selection decision to move from purchasing to development teams. For example, purchasers at one firm instruct suppliers to meet with engineers directly during advanced development projects. This firm wants to prevent advance development personnel from making early sourcing decisions before team members have the best information available.

Whatever supplier selection approach is used, reaching a consensus at some point concerning the suppliers who will become involved early in product/process development is critical. Some teams may delegate this responsibility to the sourcing member or a subgroup of the team. This individual or subgroup then has the primary responsibility for identifying and evaluating potential supply sources. Other firms use commodity management teams to identify and select suppliers.

Reaching a consensus concerning supplier selection may not be as straightforward as it sounds. Several companies recognize that purchasing and engineers must develop closer relationships and collaborate during the selection process, something that may not occur regularly. For some firms, this presents a hurdle to the integration process that must be overcome. Product and process development is often a highly technical activity demanding technical expertise. Purchasing, which offers commercial expertise, may not be fully qualified in technical aspects of product and process development. When this is the case, authority for final supplier selection may shift to engineering specialists.

CASE EXAMPLE

Engineering Priority

Several companies noted that while supplier selection should ideally be a joint activity between engineering and purchasing, engineering often exerts a stronger or dominant role in the final selection decision. Engineering performs a technical evaluation of potential suppliers, while purchasing handles final contract negotiations. A representative of a company characterized by strong internal research and development staffs maintains it is often best for purchasing managers to present available data concerning materials, costs, and suppliers and allow engineers to make the supplier selection decision. While the model suggests that consensus concerning supplier selection is important, selection may be a unilateral or technical decision that others involved in the design project must accept in order to fully involve suppliers on the NPD team.

Formally Defining Roles and Responsibilities of Buyer and Supplier

Regardless of the level of supplier involvement (for example, black box versus white box), role clarity is critical to new product development success and for involving suppliers on the NPD team. Though both the buying company and supplier may be involved in defining their respective roles, the ultimate responsibility for defining expectations—and for ensuring that the new product development process is a success—lies with the buying company. While expectations must be clear, the buying company must be careful not to micromanage the process. The buying company must provide the supplier with the responsibility and appropriate authority to meet the expectations. Methods for defining design responsibility include using a statement of work, job descriptions, and letters of understanding.

As a first step, each company must recognize the other's core competency. This often allows for the development of and concurrence about the requirements and expectations in a statement of work early in the process. Successful companies also establish and streamline non–project-specific integration guidelines for each type of supplier—black, gray, or white box.

CASE EXAMPLE

Design Sourcing Guide

A company has developed a design sourcing guide that identifies roles and responsibilities of all involved parties. The guide identifies recommended and standard parts for various applications, potential costs for these parts, recommended suppliers, and ratings of suppliers' technical competencies. The document identifies functional performance criteria in a number of areas, such as quality and reliability. Further, the document identifies expected codes of conduct for the overall project team. Suppliers are able to review the general guidelines and any information specific to their firm. Suppliers may also review their position relative to competitors, though the identities of the competitors are not revealed. This document helps the company establish broad supplier expectations prior to actual new product development.

CASE EXAMPLE

Core, Leveraged, or Build-to-Print

Another company classifies every item prior to product development as either core, leveraged, or build-to-print:

For core items, the company retains all design and development responsibility. Core items define the company's products and are fixed across all products and platforms. Examples include the power train and body styling.

Leveraged items are sourced from a supplier with full design, development, and production capabilities. The company also identifies 14 commodities that should be sourced from a supplier with full design and production capabilities. For these commodities, expectations are clearly established. Items might include seating, wiring harnesses, and interior, for example.

Build-to-print items are usually simple and involve no design responsibility for the supplier. These up-front classifications provide a high level of role clarity for both parties. However, there are still some areas where the company needs to determine the role of the supply base. For example, should the company or a supplier serve as the systems integrator for all interior components? If the interior defines what the company's product is, it will remain the company's responsibility. Although an item is core, suppliers may still be involved. The important thing is that all items are classified prior to full product development. The company also publishes two pages of guidelines which define the buyer-supplier relationship. Individual and joint roles, responsibilities, and expectations are defined for the three broad phases of a NPD effort: concept definition, program implementation, and production. This has led to a more efficient process, closer supplier relationships, and a clear understanding of roles and responsibilities.

CASE EXAMPLE

Redefining Team Structure

Another company recently developed a product that was somewhat different than its usual product line. The product was designed to incorporate new technologies, and was to be produced in much lower volumes than usual. Thus, the company used strategies and processes outside of its normal operations to achieve its goals. The company formed a core team representing design, development, engineering, manufacturing, and procurement. The team was led by a senior engineer. Responsibility for engineering was divided among a small set of teams, each with specific design duties for major systems or subsystems in the end item. Project restrictions in terms of budget and time made it important for suppliers to be responsible for detail level design specifications and development. This required delegation of responsibilities and empowerment of suppliers. The company engineers had to define their role as both managers and engineers. The engineers also had to define, with supplier involvement, the role of the supply base. Suppliers were allocated to the appropriate system, subsystem, or component level team based on their expected contributions. The clear definition of roles and responsibilities allowed the company to successfully meet program goals.

Creating Buyer-Supplier Team Permanency/Stability

Permanency of buyer-seller teams refers to the degree that NPD team strategies have become part of the organizational structure and the extent to which there is continuity in the team's composition during specific new product development efforts. Field research indicates that institutionalizing the use of buyer-seller teams will lead to greater purchased product/project outcomes. The organizational structure for firms with permanent buyer-seller teams will likely be different from firms using these teams sporadically. Firms with permanent buyer-seller product development teams often have dedicated work areas with full-time resources committed to the teams. One leading firm organizes itself around dedicated teams that support design, development, engineering, manufacturing, and procurement/supply for a particular group of products. These teams have cradle-to-grave product responsibility with no internal hand-off between functional areas.

Firms that have not made significant strides in creating a permanency of buyer-seller teams usually maintain a traditional functional structure. The traditional structure features assigning members, usually on a part-time basis, to a team outside the member's functional area. Conflicting time demands often characterize part-time team assignments. When these conflicts are serious enough, team effectiveness can suffer, even when receiving supplier support.

Firms sometimes use longer-term agreements or strategic partnerships to formalize the permanency of buyer-seller teams. These agreements often stipulate that the parties will work jointly, usually through project teams, to pursue mutually beneficial market opportunities. As the use of buyer-seller teams matures, teams should expect to assume increasingly challenging assignments. In one example, the parties to a strategic partnership agreement initially assigned tasks to their teams that had a high probability of success. The teams, formalized through a high-level strategic partnership agreement, now pursue advanced technology projects that, when successful, create new market opportunities.

CASE EXAMPLE

New Faces

Disruptions to the flow and effectiveness of teams can occur, creating performance shifts, even for permanent buyer-seller teams. Personnel turnover, promotions, changes in management, and the length of the development cycle time can influence team performance. One firm with a three to four-year product development cycle has experienced high turnover with its supplier team members. Cycle times are so long that over the duration of a project some members receive promotions or leave the company. Turnover disrupts the use of suppliers as a resource for supporting product development. The key to consistency thus should not lie in the personnel, but in the corporate culture, capabilities, and processes so that turnover effects are minimized.

CASE EXAMPLE

Restarting from Square One

Another strategic partnership featuring buyer-seller teams goes through a relearning phase whenever personnel change. Communication struggles result as personnel must become familiar with each other and develop the trust that characterized the previous relationship. Formal systems governing the relationship, such as partnership agreements and permanent buyer-seller teams, are critical. These systems help guarantee that while the participants on a team or in a relationship may change, their role within the group or the relationship does not. For many firms, however, interfirm relationships are between people as much as between companies. Personnel changes create new process learning requirements.

CASE EXAMPLE

Diffusing Learning

One leading firm has aggressively pursued the permanent use of product development teams featuring active supplier involvement. Members are selected to work together in small, tight-knit groups with clear performance targets and objectives. The company expects to transfer the experience and learning gained by team members in one product area to other product areas. After project completion, the company purposely shifts experienced team members from one product area to another to cross-fertilize ideas. Members do not simply move from one project to another within a single product area.

Using Contractual Mechanisms to Encourage Supplier Commitment

Many companies use long-term agreements (LTAs) to facilitate the supplier's involvement and commitment to the team effort. These companies view supplier relationships as a long-term business investment and an acceptable element of cost. LTAs are generally focused on key suppliers and are based on item criticality or dollar value of the purchased items. When the items are not as critical or high volume, buying companies attempt to capture the spirit of LTAs by providing preferred status to the supplier.

Buyers have become increasingly cautious in issuing LTAs because they fear becoming locked in to a supplier. Buying companies often provide long-term project-specific agreements in dynamic technology environments, while long-term commodity-specific agreements are established in more stable environments. In either situation, the effectiveness of the buying company's supplier assessment and selection process is critical for success. Buying companies may also offer LTAs within specific product lines, but multiple source within the commodity group to gain commitment while preserving a sense of supplier competition.

CASE EXAMPLE

Part Level Agreements

One company awards contracts with lifetime volume guarantees for a specific part in a specific product line, which the company indicates is really only two years. The strategy is to single-source a part number, but dual-source within the commodity family. No supplier gets the entire family. This strategy minimizes the buying company's risk by limiting the breadth of the LTA, while at the same time encouraging supplier competition (see Figure 7.2).

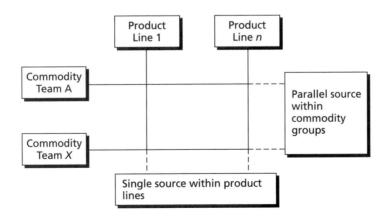

Figure 7.2. Single/multiple sourcing.

Many companies believe the supplier that is involved early should get the bulk of the production business to ensure its commitment to and involvement on the team. One company offers the integrated supplier the right of first refusal when new production orders are placed. In such instances, the supplier may also be given larger volumes in exchange for a lower price.

CASE EXAMPLE

No Long-Term Agreements

Another company used to guarantee long-term business beyond the current effort to integrated suppliers, but it is moving away from this practice. The company believes LTAs have inhibited it from accessing the latest technology or making design changes, especially during market shifts. However, it is generally understood that suppliers involved in new product development may have an initial advantage for future business. The company tends to work with incumbent suppliers for future model years. Generally, a high degree of change or unique supplier capabilities is required to switch suppliers.

CASE EXAMPLE

Separate Purchase Orders

Another company believes there is a business risk involved in putting a long-term time constraint on a contract. The company believes it is generally better to develop purchase orders that cover development costs and production costs separately. This way, though the designing firm has the upper hand on winning the production contract, there is at least an implied level of competition to drive continuous improvement.

Defining Ownership of New Product/Process Technology

Most of the companies interviewed claimed that ownership in joint development efforts should be handled on a development-by-development basis. Purchasing, research and development, and the patent office do the negotiation work to determine who will own different aspects of the new product/technology. Often, the nature of the funding determines ownership. According to one company, every time intellectual property and patent agreements are not signed, disaster is the result.

Ownership of new product/process technology is best addressed at the earliest possible stages of development. Joint patent searches, establishment of joint patents where appropriate, and the identification and documentation of intellectual property rights all address this critical issue. However, these documents and processes do not guarantee professional conduct. The buying and supplying companies must complement each other's capability to some extent, to ensure that both parties contribute to NPD success and to identify the contributions that will be made.

Suppliers have indicated in some cases that the buying company becomes too territorial about joint development efforts without proper compensation because of its buying power. A sense of equity must be established in joint development efforts, not only to drive supplier involvement on the project team and current product development success, but to promote long-term business potential as well.

CASE EXAMPLE

Patent Searches

One company makes patent investigation a major part of the discovery process. Patent investigation occurs well before actual new product (molecule) development. In the case where no patent currently exists, the company usually tries to patent a family of molecules covering all variants that may have useful biological activity. Intermediates may also be included in the patent if they are unique. This helps address the issue of ownership. However, there are times that a process developed by a supplier is patentable. In such cases, the companies develop a special agreement about intellectual property rights. Usually, the final agreement with a supplier who develops a process for the company excludes that supplier from competitive use of the process regardless of who ends up with legal ownership.

CASE EXAMPLE

We Own It!

Another company generally retains all rights to product and process design, including patents and intellectual property rights for critical components. An exception is made when the company engages in joint development work (which is not common at this point). In the case of joint development, rights are shared on a fifty-fifty basis. However, a one-year exclusivity agreement is usually imposed in such cases. Similarly, another company typically claims all patent rights when working with integrated suppliers. There is generally a timeline issued on how long the company retains sole use, depending on the product development cycle and the overall product life cycle.

JOINTLY ESTABLISH CLEAR METRICS AND TARGETS

Leading firms rely on established product/project target measurement systems that incorporate defined and understood performance metrics during product development. Sound reasons exist for establishing performance targets and measurement systems. Developing quantified targets, along with the systems to measure those targets, provides performance benchmarks against which to evaluate progress and identify problems as early as possible in the design process. Performance metrics and measurement systems support the development of team strategies and action plans, allow the team to report its progress to executive management, and enable team members to receive performance feedback. Also, teams that establish performance targets have a greater probability of success compared with teams that do not establish targets.

Target setting is an ideal way to gain commitment within a team because members will more likely commit to targets they help establish. Furthermore, if a team sets its targets properly, a clear understanding should exist among team members concerning individual accountability. Suppliers, who may be involved early in the target setting process, begin to understand their role and how they must contribute. Target setting begins to build individual and team accountability, which should promote effort and commitment.

Clearly stated performance targets reduce the likelihood that members will misunderstand what the team is trying to accomplish. Furthermore, the target setting process helps establish and clarify individual member roles. Performance targets established by teams are often more aggressive than targets established by an individual external to the team. The link between target setting and performance is such that organizations and teams cannot ignore this activity and still hope to satisfy product performance expectations. Target setting is a critical part of the group process.

CASE EXAMPLE

Milestones

Successful product development requires that teams establish cost and timing milestones as a product moves through development. A leading electronics company uses a five-phase development process with performance measurement systems to track development progress. Product development phases include (1) product/process definition, (2) integrated product/process design, (3) design execution, (4) factory deployment, and (5) stable production. While product development projects have macro targets for budget, timing, and product performance, each phase has formal reviews with measurable outputs. The development team must satisfy these output requirements before proceeding. Suppliers begin contributing during the earliest phases of development.

The level of supplier involvement, criticality and volume of procured parts, technical uncertainty and complexity, and extent of trust between the buyer and supplier often determine the process for determining targets. The exact development process is situation-specific, but black-box suppliers are generally involved from the beginning in setting targets. The buyer and supplier jointly develop these targets based on previous experience and expected business performance. The process is likely to be much more iterative for gray-box and some white-box suppliers. A combination of top-down and bottom-up techniques is used to arrive at agreeable targets. These relationships are depicted in Figure 7.3.

Although much of the discussion in this section is focused on cost, costs cannot be isolated from performance issues such as quality, features, timing, and technology. Trade-offs must be made as target costs are first developed, then negotiated. For example, along with product cost targets, achieving cycle time targets is critical. Recognizing that time to market is a key competitive success factor, most firms are establishing aggressive concept-to-

Goal: Establish and prioritize end item targets
- Performance levels and potential trade-offs defined for cost, quality, technology, schedule, etc.
Sources:
- Market analysis
- Previous similar projects and previous internal experience
- Company established minimal acceptable limits
- Closely allied supplier partners

Goal: Establish system level targets
- Joint target development with allied and preselected black-box suppliers
- Early communication with potential gray-box suppliers
- Buyer driven targets for all white-box items
Sources:
- Competitive teardowns
- Allied and preselected black-box suppliers
- Previous experience and internal expertise
- Benchmarking to competitor's suppliers

Goal: Establish subsystem and component level targets
- Delegate responsibility to allied and black-box suppliers to drive targets in their supply chains
- Support potential gray-box suppliers by identifying potential lower-level leveraged suppliers
- No further targets required for white-box items
Sources:
- Internal cross-functional teams, with extensive procurement involvement
- Bid/quotes from the supply base
- Benchmarking to competitor's suppliers
- Previous experience/internal expertise

Goal: Select suppliers and finalize targets at all levels of assembly
- Allied partners and most black-box suppliers chosen during program-planning phase
- Assess gray-box and white-box suppliers' capability and capacity to deliver to targets
- NPD core and support teams select all white-box and gray-box suppliers
- Reconcile all targets bottom up, then top down as needed
- Sign preliminary statement of work to secure contractual commitment
Sources:
- Preestablished supplier selection criteria and preapproved/certified supplier lists
- Project-specific competitive priorities list
- NPD core and support teams

Outcomes and Enablers:
- Target-driven product development
- Ensure that measurement systems are aligned with targets
- Use discipline when responding to requested target changes
- Conduct kick-off meeting with all key suppliers to generate enthusiasm, teamwork, and mutual understanding of objectives

Figure 7.3. Target driven product/process development.

market cycle-time targets. One firm tracks supplier progress closely, knowing that a delay will affect a product's launch. For example, it times the introduction of its products with a major worldwide trade show. A launch delay has serious consequences on a product's market acceptance. However, some firms rely extensively on formal cost targets as the key metric to guide product development. Most firms studied operate in intensely competitive industries. Their ability to target a cost to a specific market segment (and then meet that target) is critical to success.

CASE EXAMPLE

Setting Cost Targets

A firm that is noted for meeting its target cost relies extensively on a formalized process to develop cost targets. Target-setting, which is companywide rather than functional, recognizes that the best opportunity to improve cost, quality, and manufacturability is through new product development. The company first identifies a product sales price that will be competitive with the target market. Next, profitability targets are established that reflect corporate goals. The difference between the product sales price and desired profitability becomes the target cost.

Meeting the target cost becomes the primary responsibility of the product development team. The team breaks down the product into major systems, each of which receives an allowable system cost. Next, the team identifies the subsystems and major components within each system, along with their allowable cost. The team then works to meet overall target costs when designing subsystems and parts, doing whatever is required to adhere to the cost targets. This often requires managing trade-offs between competitive dimensions (for example, cost versus weight or speed) or reallocating costs among subsystems to meet the overall target cost. Since this firm sources most of its finished product externally, supplier involvement is extensive when developing target costs. Suppliers are typically involved one year before finalizing product drawings. During this time, the development team works with suppliers to establish cost targets for each component or subsystem. The team encourages the supplier to participate in company-sponsored value analysis exercises, as required, to help meet target costs. The fact that a 1994 product launch came within one half of 1 percent of meeting the target cost established three years earlier reflects the success of this approach.

CASE EXAMPLE

Developing Cost Expertise

A common issue in setting cost targets is the ability to target cost when using a single supplier in a partnership. Although it is a partnership, many buying companies believe it is necessary either to have internal expertise or to market test prices periodically to ensure competitive pricing. One company develops cost targets as shown in Figure 7.3. Targets are first established top-down. The end item target is established through market analysis. Then major systems are allocated targets using internal expertise and key supplier input. Finally, subsystem and component targets are established using a similar process. The company does not examine in great detail how suppliers develop their costs. As long as suppliers meet targets, they can keep their profits. If the company later finds out they are being gouged, the company will negotiate new prices.

Part of the preprogram effort also includes value analysis for each major subsystem with supplier participation in a bottom-up approach to provide a check for the top-down targets. Targets are compared and rationalized as appropriate. Any team has the ability to shift around targets within its own effort as long as it meets its allocated overall target. If needed, a team can negotiate with other teams for a larger allocation. The negotiations move up the ladder from lower to higher levels of assembly. Suppliers may be involved in target shifting negotiations within a commodity. However, they are not involved in negotiations between commodities.

Strategic planning teams set minimal acceptable worldwide customer requirements limits in a number of areas (such as weight, quality, and cost). The development team then writes a development specification using these limits as a guide. The development team can change the limit if the chief engineer can prove that target customers do not require the specified parameters. Targets must be finalized and agreed on by the buyer and supplier. A statement of work, which is generally first developed internally, must be reviewed and agreed on by the supplier. The commodity business plan actually calls for the company and the supplier to coplan the work. Though much information is shared, there are limits. For example, competition is so intense that cycle plans are not shared with suppliers. As a matter of fact, cycle plans often are not even shared within the company.

The company's overall strategy requires targets to drive the NPD effort. A paradigm shift was required for the entire team to own the targets and to realize that everybody—including suppliers—must contribute. Discipline must be used to not overdesign a product. Established targets must drive the design. If it looks like a team will not hit its targets, the team can work with other teams to negotiate for some of their resources or budget. If performance targets will not be met, product launch may be delayed rather than change the performance targets. The company actually delayed one launch for six months because performance targets were not met. After the product was finally launched, it was well accepted in the market.

In the past, and even to some extent today, both the company's engineers and the supplier's engineers in the development process looked at priorities and design issues sequentially (first concentrating on functions, then quality, weight, and cost.) If the project ran out of time, cost issues might never have been addressed. The company is moving towards Toyota engineering, which assesses all objectives at once. The statement of work identifies all assumptions and priorities. Suppliers may be asked to help identify priorities in this early stage of development.

The company's contract with all suppliers demands a 5 percent real cost reduction over time to help the company keep sales prices down. Suppliers get a long-term commitment and retain any benefits over 5 percent cost savings per annum. The company's total cost management (TCM) initiative drives supplier improvements (cost savings) and establishes an affordable business structure. TCM initiatives are not directly linked to NPD efforts. Rather, they are ongoing processes to drive continuous improvement.

CASE EXAMPLE

Rolling Cost Model

At another company, there is no formal target cost process. Customers want a solution, and the company looks at its building blocks to identify options. The company tries to meet customer cost targets by adjusting and changing the building blocks (parts). At this point, target costing is not linked back to the suppliers. The company does use a rolling cost model wherein the target cost for parts and operations are compared to the existing market prices. The product development team begins to work with the different pieces to close the gaps. This is an ongoing process, and the differences are eventually narrowed through internal or external product or process improvements.

SUMMARY

The first two steps of the supplier integration execution process, giving suppliers an active role on the project team and jointly establishing clear metrics and targets, are intended to drive buyer and supplier ownership and commitment to the NPD effort. Key points of contact are identified; direct function-to-function communication is established; roles and responsibilities are agreed on; and performance metrics are defined. As the transition point from the strategic planning phase to the execution phase, these two steps lay the groundwork for successful coordination between the buying company and its suppliers throughout the design effort.

Chapter 8

Information Sharing and Learning from Experience: The Daily Grind

"One of the biggest problems we experience is getting our engineers to accept the idea that a supplier from outside the company will be sitting in on design meetings. They simply can't get over the 'not invented here' syndrome, and feel they can't trust the supplier not to go to competitors with our designs!"

Purchasing manager, electronics manufacturer

INTRODUCTION

With suppliers' roles and responsibilities clearly established and their involvement on core or support NPD teams secured as appropriate, it is time to get down to business. The most effective and efficient NPD process is characterized by the open two-way sharing of business and technical information and the involvement of suppliers and all other cross-functional team members in decision making and problem solving. Honest and timely communication ensures that project goals are aligned, requirements and specifications understood, and progress monitored. It also facilitates better decision making and problem solving at an early stage in the NPD effort. To maximize the benefits of this open communication, it is important to allow suppliers to provide input to decisions that are jointly made and the freedom to make decisions where they have a higher level of expertise.

Having encouraged and enabled a high level of supplier involvement, it is critical to measure the specific contributions that suppliers make and how those contributions relate to the overall success of the development effort. Supplier performance metrics, which were established and agreed on during target-driven product planning, must be used throughout the development effort to ensure progress is being made and to identify and resolve potential problems as soon as possible. This chapter examines the daily activities of the NPD effort, focusing on communication, supplier involvement, and performance measures (see Figure 8.1).

SHARE INFORMATION OPENLY AND EXTENSIVELY

Much information has already been shared between the buyer and supplier to get to this point in the execution process. Customer requirements as well as cost and technological

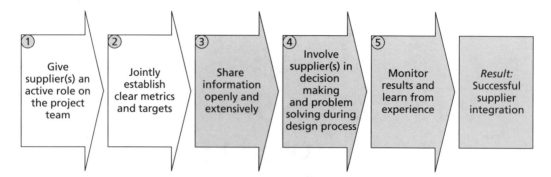

Figure 8.1. Supplier integration execution process.

data were communicated to define roles and responsibilities and to establish performance targets and metrics. If the groundwork was properly established in the early stages, information should flow freely between companies during design and development.

However, as design activities begin to pick up steam, it may be necessary to discuss technological and business issues in greater detail. Direct intercompany function-to-function communication, especially engineer-to-engineer communication, is critical to ensure that timely and accurate information is shared between parties. A high level of trust and the use of confidentiality agreements facilitates the free flow of information. When face-to-face communication is either not practical or not required, electronic linkages can be effectively used to share information. Regardless of the communication mechanism, continued information sharing is critical during the development effort to track progress, identify and solve problems early, and take advantage of new information or technology developments.

The content, level of detail provided, and the direction(s) of information flow depend on the role of the supplier as well as on the extent of use of other integrative strategies such as confidentiality agreements and long-term business agreements. Though each situation is unique, leading firms rely on a variety of methods to promote cross-functional/interfirm communication and coordination. The following information flows typify NPD efforts:

- Point-to-point interfirm communication between functional personnel

- Face-to-face meetings, including product development meetings, performance reviews, and joint target-setting meetings

- Joint teleconferences as needed or on a regularly scheduled basis

- Either temporary or permanent colocation of key design personnel

- Integrative information technology systems, such as CAD, electronic mail, groupware, intranets, and World Wide Web sites

- Use of first-tier suppliers to create communication and coordination linkages with second- and third-tier suppliers

- Use of liaison personnel dedicated to improving communication between firms

Four key communication strategies—developing trust to enable communication, confidentiality agreements, reward/risk practices, and direct cross-functional intercompany communication—are discussed in detail. Other strategies such as colocation and electronic linkages are discussed in a subsequent section, which addresses supplier involvement in decision making and problem solving.

Developing Trust to Enable Communication

Sharing information, whether it is confidential or not and regardless of whether confidentiality agreements are in place, requires trust. Fundamentally, companies develop trust through their performance over time, but the use of formal trust-building processes can help speed up the development. Formal trust-building processes may be especially critical with new suppliers, as trust has not had a chance to develop over time through a business relationship.

CASE EXAMPLE

Learn about the Other Party

In one company's most strategic and long-term supplier integration effort, there was some early resistance to information sharing from both sides due to lack of trust. As engineers and scientists shared information, each side learned about the other and opened itself to the risk of disclosure. Time was the main factor in developing trust, although the companies also tried to push things along. Partnership meetings occurred three times a year, with sites shifted between each party. Each side sent six to eight people to each partnership meeting. Each company designated a point of contact for the partnership as the person to go to if there were questions (such as what type of information could be exchanged) in the relationship. This formal control process is still in effect. However, trust is now so high that neither company feels it is necessary to follow a formal communication process.

CASE EXAMPLE

Aboveboard

According to another company, trust exists when the other company believes that you are dealing with them aboveboard and that you are living up to the agreements that have been reached (or if not, explaining why). Trust is absolutely essential—no communication occurs in the absence of trust. Companies must go through some hard times to develop the highest level of trust. If you experience only good times, the relationship and mutual trust are not tested. The company minimizes the potential for a lapse in trust by selectively integrating suppliers. The company will not work with suppliers who are direct competitors or who are suppliers to direct competitors working on similar projects.

Confidentiality Agreements

Confidentiality agreements are widely used, even when a high level of trust exists, to facilitate communication processes. These agreements protect both parties from improper business conduct on the other's part. They are generally signed prior to actual product design, as early as the idea-generation stage of the development.

CASE EXAMPLE

Build Up Trust

One company uses simple partnership charters to build trust and facilitate communication. Both parties must support these charters at the highest level. Conditions and requirements of the partnership are identified in the charter. Further, formal contracts such as letters of understanding, nondisclosure agreements, and exclusivity agreements for codeveloped materials are implemented. The legal department is involved in developing nondisclosure agreements. After agreements are signed, training occurs at the company to educate employees about the partnership and its details.

CASE EXAMPLE

Protect Interests

Conversely, another company routinely uses nondisclosure agreements to protect each party's interests. The agreement is defined in the company's general contract, which it signs with suppliers prior to the start of design work or any other transactions. The general contract also requires the supplier to obtain permission from the company if the supplier intends to apply for a patent on technology developed as a result of the relationship with the company. The general contract is followed by a more specific agreement as the two companies enter into actual design and development activities.

CASE EXAMPLE

Commit Volumes

Another company protects supplier technology rights through various mechanisms. However, the business relationship really holds the key to open communication and sharing of ideas. If the company is interested in the supplier's technology, it will commit a specific volume level to the supplier, after which there is full information sharing with the company's internal suppliers for competitive purposes. The company also cautions suppliers that once a product is introduced, competitors do a complete teardown of the product (reverse engineer it), so it is difficult to keep any innovation protected.

CASE EXAMPLE

No Lock-Ins

Another company has traditionally not used confidentiality agreements with suppliers, but this is changing. The company is finding that it is having to disclose more information about the entire product to suppliers of individual components in order to facilitate the design. However, nondisclosure agreements still are not used for technology sharing in early stages of product development. Particularly if the company is working on a similar technology internally, it does not want to be locked into letting a supplier develop a promising technology.

CASE EXAMPLE

Involve the Lawyers Early

In one company, confidentiality is seen as part of the supplier/buyer business relationship, though only two confidentiality agreements were signed in the most recent extensive development effort. Typically, the development team has legal department encouragement in the early stages of a development to implement formal confidentiality contracts. However, many teams feel that legal agreements are restrictive and can prevent innovation/creativity. Protection can become a restraint.

CASE EXAMPLE

Become the Customer of Choice

Another company also traditionally did not require specific confidentiality agreements with its key suppliers. The company works closely with suppliers to become the customer of choice. The company has high expectations of its suppliers and has not had confidentiality problems. It does however, take preventive measures, such as restricting release of drawings and documents on a need-to-know basis

The extent of use and details of confidentiality agreements depends on the existing level of trust, length of previous relationship, and level of involvement. While the majority of companies agree that confidentiality agreements are important, they also feel that such agreements do little to enhance business performance without trust. The reinforcing relationship between trust and formal confidentiality agreements, and their mutual effect on the buyer-supplier relationship, is depicted in Figure 8.2.

Reward/Risk Practices

Some new product development efforts meet expectations; some exceed expectations; and some fall far below expectations. How should a supplier be rewarded when its performance

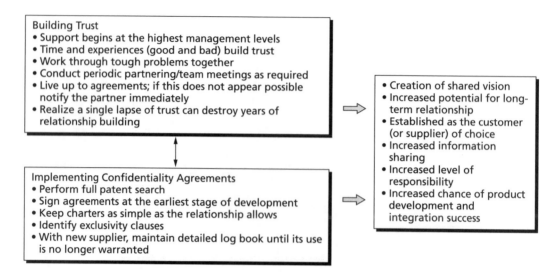

Figure 8.2. Relationship between trust, confidentiality agreements, and relationship.

exceeds expectations in terms of time, cost, and production volumes? How should the supplier reward the buyer when volume projections are exceeded? Should suppliers absorb costs when volumes are less than projected even though the problem may simply be a bad forecast provided by the buyer? Who pays for the cost of design changes? What happens when a technology simply does not pan out?

Successful companies proactively address these issues. Either through formal contractual agreements or less formal letters of understanding, up-front agreements on the rewards and risks of the development effort define the course of action based on an evaluation of results. Such risk/reward sharing agreements provide all parties with confidence that open and timely sharing of information is in their best interests. Some generalizable observations from the interviews on how companies share risks and rewards include the following:

- Link development competition with commercialization

- Compensate suppliers for shelving their technology, or release claims to the technology to avoid the risk of losing supplier input into future advanced development

- Agree to volumes within negotiated pricing formulas

- Agree on alternatives if the supplier is not able to meet its obligations (for example, penalties or switching costs)

- Having the buying company accept risk and pay for changes driven or mandated internally

- Allow the supplier the fair profit it needs to invest in the company and pay stakeholders

- Focus on cost drivers and final customer value rather than the supplier's final price to drive continuous improvement

- Share pain equally if volume falls short of projection

- Expect continuous improvement (in cost, quality, features, and so on) based on preestablished improvement parameters if volume exceeds projection

CASE EXAMPLE

Pricing Formula

One company and its suppliers agree to volumes within a pricing formula and foreign exchange agreements when appropriate. Company-driven changes are readily paid for by the company, rather than having the supplier taking on the cost and risk. As a check/control, price/cost analyses are undertaken to ensure the effect is reasonable. Finance works closely with procurement. Both work towards meeting the vehicle target price even through design changes.

CASE EXAMPLE

We're Responsible

Another company provides volume projections to suppliers and is fully responsible for market acceptance of the new products. For example, if the company offers rebates, it will absorb all the costs. If actual volumes are still less than projected, pain is shared equally between the company and its suppliers. There is no formal plan for the case when actual volumes exceed projections, but it appears that the company will be more likely in the future to consistently pursue reduced costs when volumes exceed projections.

CASE EXAMPLE

Cost/Volume Benefits

Another company fully benefits from any and all cost savings the supplier comes up with. Consequently, there is little motivation for the supplier to work at reducing costs. However, the supplier expects to receive greater future volumes as a result of value engineering activities, as the company will give the supplier a preferred status and a higher priority in future business decisions.

Direct Cross-Functional/Intercompany Communication

Cross-functional/intercompany communication linkages are key to effective communication. Without efficient and effective communication during product development, firms can expect reduced purchased product and project outcomes. The traditional model of buyer-seller communication featuring purchasing and sales as the focus of intercompany communication is obsolete. Once a supplier begins to provide early product design support, communication must flow between technical specialists as well. Communication linkages become point-to-point rather than channeled through a functional group such as purchasing.

The issue of establishing communication channels not involving purchasing, however, is a concern at some firms. This concern relates to improper commitments or decisions that personnel external to purchasing might make during the communication process. One leading firm has actively educated cross-functional personnel about the authority they have (and do not have) and the role they play during interfirm communication.

CASE EXAMPLE

Technical Exchanges

While engineer-to-engineer technical communication is common during product development, one leading firm is attempting to expand cross-functional communication linkages as a means to develop closer buyer-supplier relationships. Much of the communication occurring today involves technical personnel discussing specific tasks or projects. As the firm identifies new performance opportunities through its strategic supplier relationships, it must manage work processes that are organizational and behavioral rather than technical. Many technical people, however, do not want to become involved with nontechnical issues. Supplier managers, who are predominantly technical specialists, probably cannot manage the growth of strategic relationships. This firm is seeking to develop communication linkages outside technical areas.

INVOLVE SUPPLIER(S) IN DECISION MAKING AND PROBLEM SOLVING DURING DESIGN PROCESS

With the supplier established as part of the project team (step 1 of the execution process), it would seem that involving the supplier in decision making and problem solving during design would be a natural process. However, even when strategic planning and up-front tactical moves have been made to ensure supplier involvement, it is often during actual design that the "not invented here" syndrome retrenches itself. Engineers who either were reluctant to integrate suppliers to begin with or are exposed to new supplier technologies and processes in the face of meeting short development times tend to "shadow engineer" or disregard supplier inputs altogether as crunch time approaches.

It is important during actual design and development to continue to involve suppliers in decision making and problem solving for a variety of reasons. First, this leads to the most efficient use of resources. A lot of time, effort, and money was put into identifying supplier integration opportunities, selecting suppliers, defining roles, and so on. To ensure that effort was not wasted, suppliers must have input in those areas in which they are expected to contribute. Second, supplier involvement in design decisions leads to the most effective use of resources. The supplier has been selected and integrated based on the premise that it has certain capabilities outside of the buying firm's core capabilities that will contribute to customer satisfaction. Without allowing the supplier to contribute in those areas where it is the expert, a suboptimal design will result. Finally, by involving suppliers in decision making, they can be more effectively held accountable for meeting their obligations.

CASE EXAMPLE

Face-to-Face Meetings

Most firms we studied recognize the potential benefit of involving suppliers during the design phase of new product development. Leading firms take different approaches when involving strategic suppliers during the actual design process. One firm, noted for relying extensively on its suppliers for design support, establishes offsite facilities where supplier engineers work side-by-side with the purchaser's engineers. During early phases of a project, this firm prefers face-to-face team communication about the use of information technology to support its integration efforts. While the company relies on integrative systems technology during later phases of development, it promotes personal interaction and brainstorming early in development.

A recent project at this company featured product development team meetings held every two weeks—meetings that suppliers sometimes led. A primary objective of these meetings was the exchange of information between internal team members and suppliers. The product development team committed one-third of the meeting to issues involving the buyer and its suppliers. As the development project progressed, these meetings evolved from planning and brainstorming sessions to problem-solving and information-sharing forums. Suppliers even became involved with design studio personnel with few constraints placed on their participation. The purchaser encouraged suppliers to contribute fully, a role that made some suppliers uncomfortable. Suppliers had first sight of the design and adopted "some of the passion for the design." This example highlights the need for selecting suppliers who are willing to contribute throughout product conceptualization and design. It also illustrates the need for selecting suppliers who can comfortably challenge the buying company's product designers.

CASE EXAMPLE

Elicit Ideas

Another company uses value analysis to involve suppliers in decision making and to select supplier value. The company developed an internal formal process for cost improvement. Suppliers must periodically complete a form identifying cost or process improvement ideas. The forms are routed to purchasing for logging, then directed to the appropriate engineering group. If the supplier's idea is rejected and it is over a certain dollar amount, rejection must be signed off on by appropriate management personnel. If the idea is accepted, the company and supplier share the rewards. Part of the supplier's quarterly rating involves whether it provided improvement ideas.

Many companies identified colocation and linked information systems as two key strategies to facilitate supplier involvement in decision making and problem resolution. These two strategies are discussed in detail below.

Colocation of Design Personnel

Colocation of personnel facilitates supplier participation on product/project teams. Once a firm decides to include suppliers in product development, a next step often involves colocating personnel at the buyer's or supplier's facility. Colocation refers to assigning personnel from a buyer or supplier to work at the other party's facilities day-to-day, temporarily, or for the duration of a project. Field research with leading firms supports a number of points relating to the colocation of design or other personnel.

Colocation to support new product development is rarely permanent. While permanent colocation is sometimes used to support JIT II operational requirements, product development is usually project-oriented. This means that the project has defined starting and ending dates, with the duration of colocation often depending on the length of the project. Also, a supplier may provide onsite support only during certain phases of a project, such as concept or design development. The supplier may be part of the product development team with a physical working area at the purchaser's location. An often cited duration for colocation is one to two weeks at a time, although colocation can be for the entire length of the development project.

CASE EXAMPLE

Continuous Colocation

Colocation of supplier design personnel can be continuous. One supplier who is pursuing closer buyer-supplier interaction has permanently colocated one of its designers at its customer's facility. This designer, who is experienced and knows the purchaser's personnel well, resides full-time at an off-site location working with the buyer's design engineers. Union restrictions prohibit onsite colocation. Another firm is providing one or two people full time at a purchaser's site to help formulate and recommend plastic materials during new product development. The two firms recently entered a corporatewide agreement that should result in greater interaction between the firms.

Colocation does not have to occur only at a purchaser's facilities. Design engineers or other personnel may move between facilities to reduce the burden and expense on one party. This is the case with a leading firm working on advanced technology development projects with a specific supplier. The parties alternate week-long visits of personnel between the purchaser and the supplier. Alternating colocation sites requires that each party have the facilities and equipment required to support the process.

Information technology systems may reduce the need to colocate design or other personnel. Conflicting viewpoints exist concerning the use of information systems technology as a substitute for physically colocating personnel. A firm noted for its progressive approach to supplier integration argues that information systems, while critical, are not substitutes for face-to-face interaction, particularly during the early phases of a project. Colocation supports (1) increased informal interaction, (2) enhanced role clarity and understanding, (3) more frequent communication between the parties, (4) development of positive relationships, (5) faster decision making and problem solving, and (6) enhanced creative thinking from working together physically. This is critical during early phases of a project when teams make decisions that affect later development efforts and total project costs.

CASE EXAMPLE

Virtual Colocation

One firm we studied aggressively pursues what it terms "virtual colocation" using state-of-the-art integrative systems technology. Interactive computer-aided-design systems with videoconferencing through personal computers provide effective virtual colocation. While still relying on physical colocation during the early phases of a project or when problems require joint solution, integrated systems eliminate much of the need for supplier colocation throughout the NPD effort. However, nonintegrated information technology systems will still lead to "throwing the design over the wall from one company to another."

Some firms have yet to practice internal colocation during product development. When product development is an individual's primary responsibility, colocation of team members often occurs during some or all of the project. When team assignments are part-time, members usually maintain their permanent job location, which limits the amount of internal colocation that occurs. A major consumer products company addressed this issue, at least partly, by internally colocating purchasing with research and development personnel. Without internal colocation, purchasing managers must rely on research and development to keep them informed of product and process developments, which overall has not worked well. We can speculate that firms that do not practice internal colocation during product development will be less likely to practice supplier colocation.

Some firms perceive that limited value exists in colocating supplier personnel. The consumer products company cited above does not practice colocation with suppliers. It argues that each supplier is doing something different with unique types of equipment, labs, procedures, and so on. Some managers perceive that colocating with suppliers would add minimally, if at all, to the product development process. A leading Japanese electronics firm maintains that the communication required between the company and its suppliers during product development does not warrant colocation of supplier personnel. A second Japanese firm suggested that while the frequency of colocating supplier personnel has increased over the past five years, this trend will not continue. Some managers believe that the buying company will get too close to colocated suppliers, making it difficult to replace them if the situation warrants a change. Furthermore, colocating suppliers may place proprietary information at risk.

Strong union contracts can be a barrier to placing a supplier's personnel on site. Unionized contracts covering product designers can present a major hurdle to supplier colocation. A leading proponent of colocating suppliers was forced to establish offsite locations to colocate design personnel. Trade union restrictions prohibited suppliers from working at the company's design center.

Colocation applies to a limited number of suppliers. Several firms suggested that colocation should be a selective option. Expecting to colocate dozens of suppliers to support a development project is not feasible. This makes the supplier colocation decision critical because most projects will involve only a few key suppliers. Some suppliers do not want a colocation arrangement while others are willing to pursue this approach. Selecting suppliers for colocation is a decision with strategic implications. One company goes so far as to certify that a supplier's engineers are technically competent before allowing them to work on product and process development.

In selected cases colocation can involve customers. A worldwide high-technology leader colocates with key customers during portions of the product development process. During design reviews, for example, the goal is to ensure that not only are the preidentified customer requirements being properly addressed, but also that new options identified by the NPD team are evaluated for their added value. In some cases, the customer is involved in prototype tests as well, to ensure that requirements are actually being met.

Linked Information Systems

Linked information systems between the buyer and seller are increasingly being used to facilitate communication of both technical and business information. These systems also serve to keep the supplier involved in decision making and problem solving throughout the design effort. However, developing common linkages for use during the design and development stage of NPD has not been easy. For example, the myriad of different CAD systems in use means that data transfer is often not seamless. Files must be converted to neutral formats before transmitting. Both buying and supplying firms realize the importance and potential advantages of linked systems, but the lack of industry standards creates a barrier to implementation.

Companies that have established long-term relationships or strategic alliances with suppliers are often more successful at aligning the suppliers' information systems technology with their own. The buying company often focuses on integrating systems with its key suppliers first and then working through the value chain. However, new suppliers, or suppliers identified as potential partners by the buying company, may have already invested in their information systems. These new suppliers are unlikely to be able to justify investment in new information systems without a long-term commitment from the buying company.

The majority of the companies we interviewed did have EDI systems linked with key suppliers for transaction processing during the production phase of a NPD effort. E-mail, computer-coded faxing, and the use of the Internet are increasingly being used to share information.

CASE EXAMPLE

Single Standard

One company has adopted a single CAD standard for the company. The company does business with many suppliers who use a different standard. This can lead to difficulties in sharing design information electronically. Translation or conversion attempts are not 100 percent effective. The company has attempted to push some suppliers to adopt its standard, but expense is a barrier. In some cases, the company has negotiated with a supplier to amortize the expense of adopting a new system over the piece price of components. Even with those suppliers who use compatible CAD systems, the company has not found electronic linkage to be a substitute for colocation. Although the data can be exchanged easily enough, face-to-face contact is important for involving suppliers in decision making and problem solving.

CASE EXAMPLE

Uses EDI

Another company makes very limited use of electronic transfer of design data. However, the company does make extensive use of E-mail for problem solving and information sharing. The company also uses EDI to share updated project schedules, forecasts, and design release information with key suppliers. The company has started down an evolutionary path to increase the use of linked information systems for design data. The company plans to use integrated CAD selectively on a case-by-case basis to work out the bugs and measure its value.

CASE EXAMPLE

Link to Web Site

Another company is just now increasing its use of electronic linkages to transmit design data. The company plans to transmit top level drawings to suppliers via the Internet. The company also maintains a Web site on the Internet for order transmission and reviewing supplier literature. However, there are barriers to further system integration with suppliers. For example, the company has to evaluate whether the benefits of system integration justify the costs. The company knows that a lot of time and effort will be required to make the system integration happen, especially since it has very long supply chains.

CASE EXAMPLE

Interactive CAD

Another company wants to develop supplier relationships so that suppliers are seamless extensions of the company. Both colocation and electronic linkages are tactics to

(continued)

achieve this type of relationship. The company's suppliers would like to see an industrywide standard developed for CAD, but major players in the industry have standardized internally on different systems. The lack of an industry standard is more of a problem for smaller suppliers; larger suppliers can accommodate multiple standards. Where the company is able to use a common CAD system with a supplier, interactive CAD combined with video conferencing has created a type of virtual colocation.

MONITOR RESULTS AND LEARN FROM EXPERIENCE

Performance must be measured throughout the development effort. Equally important is a performance assessment after the design is complete, as well as performance monitoring during ramp-up and volume production. By conducting postaudits, both the buying company and supplier will have feedback to identify continuous improvement opportunities. It is important that performance measures are not used simply to assign blame. The measures should be used to drive the development effort, encourage continuous improvement, celebrate victories, jointly identify and resolve potential problems, and, in the case of continued nonperformance, provide justification for terminating the relationship.

Performance Measures

Most firms still rely on traditional performance metrics when evaluating NPD performance. Typical product development measures include various indicators of quality, cycle time, manufacturability of design, and budget performance. Increasingly, leading firms are establishing a strategically selected set of nontraditional metrics to complement the traditional measures. Such measures are project-specific and even supplier-specific and are aimed at identifying the true value added of the extensive effort of integrating suppliers. For example, leading companies often measure the number of standardized parts used in a new product and explicitly assess the number of standard parts that suppliers used in their designs. Specifying standard rather than custom-designed components can reduce design costs and time, provide lower unit costs, and deliver known levels of quality performance.

Using numerous and various performance metrics is not the key to success. As a matter of fact, using a lot of measures can actually confound issues, indicate a lack of focus, take critical resources away from "doing" by allocating them to "measuring," and place unnecessary pressure on the doers by constantly looking over their shoulders. All measures should have a definite purpose tied to improving the NPD effort. Successful performance metrics may be characterized by the following attributes:

- Relevant: make sure metrics are based on competitive priorities

- Selective: keep the number of metrics to a minimum

- Understandable: use metrics that are clearly defined and easy to understand

- Acceptable: achieve suppliers' buy-in to metrics (and targets) early on

Table 8.1 provides a listing of product and process related NPD performance measures. The list is not meant to be exhaustive. Rather, it focuses on supplier performance measures that directly relate to the overall success of the NPD effort.

Table 8.1. NPD supplier performance measures.

Product Metrics
Purchase price cost
Quality
Performance (e.g., weight, size, etc.)
Supplier cost reduction/design improvement suggestions made and implemented
Timing and availability of prototypes
Number of supplier-related engineering change orders to the supplied item (differentiate between continuous improvement ECOs and noncompliance ECOs)
Number of supplier-related engineering change orders to other items (differentiate between continuous improvement ECOs and noncompliance ECOs)
Number of requests for increased budget
Standardization (number of reuse parts)
Technology access (time to bring new technology to market)

Process Metrics
Development costs at key milestones
Development costs at completion
Number of development milestones met
Final development milestone met
Supplier cost reduction/design improvement suggestions made and implemented
Number of supplier-related engineering change orders to the supplier's process (differentiate between continuous improvement ECOs and noncompliance ECOs)
Number of supplier related engineering change orders to other processes (differentiate between continuous improvement ECOs and noncompliance ECOs)
Time required for ramp-up to volume production
Constancy or stability of supplier NPD team members
Responsiveness to request for information (timely response)
Number (percentage) of lower-level certified suppliers used

Transfer of learning from team to team and project to project is critical for driving continuous improvement. One organization conducts lessons learned sessions after the completion of each project. The team, including any suppliers that participated with the team, analyzes each phase of a project and identifies lessons learned from the outcome. The firm transmits these lessons electronically to other project teams to accelerate the organizational rate of learning and to avoid the same problems from occurring in other projects.

Problem Resolution Practices

One of the key supplier integration success factors is resolving problems that are detected through performance monitoring, then documenting the problem and resolution to avoid similar problems in the future. Many companies attempt to resolve problems before they occur by clearly defining expectations and establishing a strong business relationship. However, conflicts do arise, so successful companies plan a proper course of action for resolving issues. The key is to focus on preestablished targets, measures, and the statement of work to assign primary responsibility—not blame—for problem resolution. To assign responsibility, both companies must work together in root cause analysis. And even with responsibility assigned, companies must work collaboratively to find an equitable solution. If trade-offs are required to resolve the problem, start trade-offs from the lowest level of assembly and work upward. Numerous companies identify key decision makers or an ombudsman to resolve issues. If issues can not be resolved at the project level, companies must be able to professionally agree to disagree and move the search for resolution up the management chain as appropriate.

CASE EXAMPLE

Reopener Clause

One company uses business agreements with reopener clauses for poor performance. Poor performance may be defined as poor quality, poor service, noncompetitive price/cost, or the like. The company strives to ensure that a supplier will not be discarded every time there is a problem. The company works with the supplier to solve problems. The company is now compiling a lessons learned database to help resolve problems with late delivery, unreliable performance, cost overruns, and so on. The information is not only used for supplier performance evaluation, it also provides feedback to all suppliers for continuous improvement. This database was developed because the company believes that all work processes need study and revision. The company needs to have the engineering project team work with suppliers to prevent problems from occurring (using the lessons learned information) or to work together in root cause analysis when problems do arise.

CASE EXAMPLE

Internal Process Benchmarks

Another company had the in-house capability to produce a product that was currently being supplied by an integrated supplier. Since the company had internal capabilities, it knew the costs associated with design, development, and manufacture. The supplier could not meet the estimated costs of the internal process. The companies worked together and shared information to resolve the issue. The company explained its internal process to the supplier. The company also agreed to deliver reliable month-to-month production schedules, which enabled efficient planning, larger volumes, and level production scheduling.

CASE EXAMPLE

Lowballing

Most companies realize that some suppliers play games. Though suppliers are involved early and help develop targets, at some point they may try to change the targets. If a supplier had previously agreed to targets, it should be held to its word. Most companies also have a pretty good idea when a supplier may be lowballing estimates to win business. In one example, a company felt strongly that a supplier was bidding low but awarded them the contract anyway. The supplier overran the agreed-on target by $100 per piece part. The company gave back $20, but the remaining $80 is still under negotiation.

SUMMARY

All of the preplanning and team structuring efforts will yield benefits only if the internal NPD team openly shares information and involves suppliers in decision making and problem solving. These processes require a high level of mutual trust that is built through experience and formal mechanisms. Confidentiality agreements, colocation strategies, and integrated information systems are frequently identified enablers/facilitators of these processes. Open and timely communication ensures that all parties are working toward the right objectives and drives better decision making. Joint problem solving and decision making based on frequent and open communication allows for the best decisions to be made, maximizes the effectiveness and efficiency of resources, and drives supplier commitment and responsibility in the NPD effort.

Performance must be monitored from the first stage the supplier is involved and throughout continuous improvement efforts in production. Measures should be focused on key performance areas, target driven, and understood and agreed on by the buying and supplying company. Real-time updates on supplier and overall NPD efforts allows for early problem identification and provides momentum when milestones are met. A postaudit with suppliers will identify lessons learned and opportunities for improvement. The results of all postaudits should be documented and shared with other internal teams to create a learning organization.

Chapter 9

Barriers to Effective Supplier Integration and Future Directions

"The barriers are tremendous; the potential benefits are even greater."

Purchasing manager

INTRODUCTION

"Where there's a will there's a way." This thought should be kept in mind by any champion of supplier integration into NPD because barriers abound that will test the fortitude of even the most ardent proponent of integration. Though all business processes face implementation challenges, the supplier integration process may be one of the most difficult to implement because it affects numerous internal and external stakeholders and encounters a web of barriers. This chapter provides information about

- Major problems encountered by firms in successfully integrating suppliers into new product development (NPD)

- Key strategies to be used in the future to overcome these problems

OVERVIEW OF BARRIERS AND SOLUTIONS

Two hundred and ninety-five responses were used as the basis for discussion. Barriers were first grouped into eight major categories. Then, each category was classified as either a strategic or an operational barrier. The resulting discussion framework is presented in Figure 9.1.

As the framework suggests, even though there is some independence of barriers, there is also a high degree of interdependence between and among the strategic and operational barriers. Solutions for strategic planning barriers must be developed for long-term effectiveness because they provide direction for supplier integration and they minimize or even eliminate operational barriers. However, even with strategic barriers resolved, operational problems arise because people who may or may not have the skills or willingness to make supplier integration happen are often charged with carrying out the process. Every businessperson is aware that the stated policy is not always the practiced policy, so operational

Strategic	⬅➡	Operational
☐ **Cultural Alignment (61)** • Resistance to change (16) • "Not invented here" syndrome (39) • Nonsupportive organizational structure (4) • Loyalty to suppliers (2) ☐ **Trust (41)** • Lack of confidence in performance (21) • Ethical conduct concerns (20) ☐ **Integrated Supply Chain Process (51)** • No formal supplier integration process (24) • Ineffective supplier selection (27) ☐ **Management Commitment (16)** • No management support or buy-in (buyer and/or supplier) (16)		☐ **Program/Project Goal Alignment (35)** • No goal alignment (16) • Ill-defined roles and responsibilities (16) • Intrusive customer involvement (3) ☐ **Honest and Effective Communication (21)** • Verbal communication problems (11) • Electronic communication issues (10) ☐ **Integration Problems (26)** • No internal cross-functional integration (13) • Supplier integration challenges (7) • Meeting customer requirements (6) ☐ **Competitive Concerns (33)** • Price pressures (11) • Risk and reward sharing (19) • Design standardization (3)

Note: Numbers in parenthesis represent the number of times an issue was reported as a problem.

Figure 9.1. Barriers to supplier integration.

barriers must be resolved. The resolution of operational problems may also be used to reevaluate and reformulate strategic initiatives.

The interrelationship and independence of strategic and operational barriers present both a major challenge and a blessing. Independence means that the supplier integration process must be constantly evaluated and managed at strategic and operational levels. However, interrelationship suggests that by focusing on perhaps a few critical strategies and formalized processes (that are likely to be firm- or industry-specific), operational and strategic barriers can be simultaneously addressed as suggested in Figure 9.2.

The bottom line is that effective supplier integration is difficult to realize due to both strategic and operational barriers. However, a solution for one problem may resolve or mitigate other problems so that, through effective planning and measurement, the likelihood of supplier integration and project success is greatly increased.

STRATEGIC PLANNING BARRIERS

Cultural Alignment

"Old habits die hard." This is especially true when it comes to supplier integration into NPD. Cultural issues were the most frequently reported problem by responding companies. Though many respondents seemed to have trouble identifying specific problems with culture—other than to say that culture was a problem—the general theme of all responses in this category appears to be fear of change and loss of control. Engineers were most often associated with resistance to change, which may be expected since the supplier is being integrated into their territory. Respondents also indicated that suppliers are at times uncomfortable with their new role as a partner in the development process.

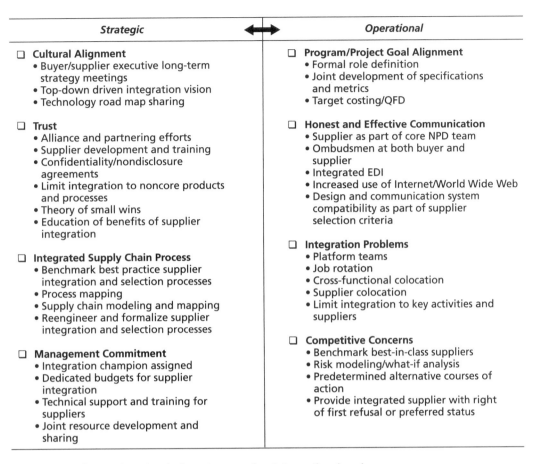

Strategic		Operational
❑ **Cultural Alignment** • Buyer/supplier executive long-term strategy meetings • Top-down driven integration vision • Technology road map sharing		❑ **Program/Project Goal Alignment** • Formal role definition • Joint development of specifications and metrics • Target costing/QFD
❑ **Trust** • Alliance and partnering efforts • Supplier development and training • Confidentiality/nondisclosure agreements • Limit integration to noncore products and processes • Theory of small wins • Education of benefits of supplier integration		❑ **Honest and Effective Communication** • Supplier as part of core NPD team • Ombudsmen at both buyer and supplier • Integrated EDI • Increased use of Internet/World Wide Web • Design and communication system compatibility as part of supplier selection criteria
❑ **Integrated Supply Chain Process** • Benchmark best practice supplier integration and selection processes • Process mapping • Supply chain modeling and mapping • Reengineer and formalize supplier integration and selection processes		❑ **Integration Problems** • Platform teams • Job rotation • Cross-functional colocation • Supplier colocation • Limit integration to key activities and suppliers
❑ **Management Commitment** • Integration champion assigned • Dedicated budgets for supplier integration • Technical support and training for suppliers • Joint resource development and sharing		❑ **Competitive Concerns** • Benchmark best-in-class suppliers • Risk modeling/what-if analysis • Predetermined alternative courses of action • Provide integrated supplier with right of first refusal or preferred status

Figure 9.2. Interrelated solutions to supplier integration barriers.

The key to driving change in culture appears to be providing evidence that supplier integration creates a "win-win-win-win" situation. Customers win by receiving products and services that meet or exceed their requirements. The company wins through increased productivity and profitability. The supplier wins through increased business opportunities with the buyer. And perhaps most important for driving cultural change, engineering as well as other functional units win through their direct linkage to the core competencies of the firm. Four subcategories of the cultural alignment problem are discussed in the following sections.

Resistance to Change. Resistance to change is a common problem in many organizations. Resistance may come from any functional area, especially when implementing systemwide processes such as supplier integration into NPD, implementing just-in-time purchasing/manufacturing, or developing a global sourcing strategy. People have a tendency to stick to the traditional processes and experiences that do not appear to need to be fixed. Resistance to change, by either the buyer or supplier, makes cultural alignment difficult. Specific problem statements included the following:

- Traditional views and corporate culture will not allow change.

- The company cannot get out of its box and realize that suppliers can bring fresh ideas.

- Internally, many people highlight past problems with suppliers rather than potential advantages of supplier integration.

- Suppliers' management shows limited flexibility to adapt to new and different methods of development.

Strategic planning and achieving a series of small wins over time were the most frequently identified potential solutions. Specific solutions included the following:

- Conduct high-level meetings with appropriate buyer and supplier executives to drive business and technological alignment prior to initiation of new projects.

- Form alliances with key suppliers and develop short-term, intermediate-term, and long-term goals for the business relationship.

- Provide education and training at both buyer and supplier companies regarding the process and benefits of supplier integration.

- Conduct ongoing formal and informal communication with potential suppliers regarding market and technology trends by holding open-houses and supplier days.

- Select initial supplier integration efforts that are low risk to demonstrate success and build momentum for change.

The Not-Invented-Here Syndrome. The not-invented-here syndrome, as reported by participating companies, seems to be driven by two forces. First is the buying company's corporate, business unit, or functional level belief that they have significant development capabilities and thus can provide a superior product without supplier integration. Second is the desire to maintain control—especially by the engineering group—of all design and development responsibilities. The desire to maintain control may be directly tied to the belief that the best capabilities reside in-house, but it also may be driven by fear that jobs will be lost, skills will be diminished, or a combination of the three. Specific problem statements included the following:

- There is a lack of recognition for the need for supplier integration.

- A very strong technical group tends to discount those items that they did not develop.

- The belief persists that if it is not made here, the product's quality and reliability will suffer.

- Management is willing to relinquish control, but operational level personnel are not willing to relinquish control, so they resist outside ideas to influence the design.

- Product development personnel fear they will lose their technical know-how and their jobs.

Common solutions were identified for the not-invented-here problem regardless of the driver of the problem. Many of the solutions were similar to those for the resistance-to-change problem. That is, it is necessary to show the benefits of supplier integration to all parties involved and to allow time for relationships to develop. Other solutions included formalizing supplier integration into the NPD process, clearly defining the buying firm's core competencies, and selecting only best-in-class suppliers. Specific solutions included:

- Clearly define and communicate the company's core competencies to all personnel so that it is understood where supplier integration should be used. Maintain internal control on strategic components, leaving freedom for supplier integration in lower-level subsystems.

- Have engineering, program management, materials management, and senior management from both companies attend a product development seminar to educate them on the how-to and benefits of supplier integration.

- Educate employees about the added value of integration, and assure the employees that they will continue to work on core/added-value jobs.

- Form a multifunctional team with technology groups to develop a process for integrating suppliers.

- A strong push from the top down is required to have engineers justify why supplier inputs can or should not be implemented. Before, the supplier was expected to justify requests for increased integration.

- Set up supplier integration efforts on a small scale with guaranteed success to change attitudes through demonstrated results. As suppliers demonstrate their technical and design capabilities, confidence about relinquishing control will develop.

- Evaluate suppliers by their competence and effect on company competitiveness, rather than by size or turnover potential. Identify and select the most technically advanced suppliers rather than the cheapest suppliers.

- Institute recognition programs that reward the use of supplier integration.

Nonsupportive Organizational Structure. Nonsupportive organizational structures such as bureaucratic lines of reporting were not frequently reported problems. There are numerous potential explanations for this. First, respondents may have implicitly included organization structure as part of their organizational culture problems. Second, participating companies may have reengineered their structures and processes so that the organizational structure now supports new initiatives such as supplier integration into NPD. Finally, functional units may have learned how to operate around and despite the system.

Regardless, companies that reported this problem indicate that it is real and significant. Solutions focused on reengineering organizational structures to allow clean lines of communication, decision making at the appropriate (lower) levels, and time to build up trust across all levels and functions. For example, the often-reported gap between engineering and purchasing can be bridged through (1) technical direction driven from the top down, (2) formalized process requiring early supplier involvement in NPD, (3) formalized process requiring purchasing review and approval of all preliminary and final bills of material, and (4) implementing platform and project team structures.

Loyalty to Suppliers. Two Pacific Rim respondents indicated that over the years they have developed strong relationships with their suppliers, built on trust and the unspoken understanding that, as long as both parties met their obligations, there would be a continued business relationship. There was concern that supplier integration into NPD would lead to a reduction in suppliers, not due to lack of performance but because supplier integration often drives supply-base reductions as buying companies align themselves and their suppliers in a virtual supply chain.

Both respondents indicated that the solution was either to develop alternative opportunities for suppliers to maintain the business relationship with the buying firm or to help the supplier develop new business relationships with other buyers. There is risk in the latter process. One respondent indicated that he helped one of his suppliers develop a high-performing, self-sustaining management structure so that the supplier could develop business with other buyers. When the supplier was called on for future business, the company found that the supplier no longer placed a high priority on its orders because the supplier was no longer dependent on the company for business.

Trust

Trust, or lack thereof, was a frequently reported problem. It also appears to be one of the most difficult problems to define and resolve. Two interdependent aspects to the trust problem emerged from the responses. First, there is often a lack of confidence that the supplier (buyer) actually has the capability and commitment to perform to the agreed-on technical specifications and business contracts. The root cause seems to be the not-invented-here syndrome, which drives a belief that "others can't perform to our level" or that "suppliers do not commit the necessary resources to our project." Second, many firms expressed concern that the supplier (buyer) will not conduct themselves ethically even with formal/legal business contracts in place. Fears of broken confidentiality agreements and improper use of proprietary information are major hurdles to successful supplier integration into NPD.

Lack of Confidence in Performance. Lack of confidence is characterized by concern about whether the supplier can and will meet commercial and technical requirements. It is a concern even if both parties are approaching the integration effort from a "win-win" perspective, and it may become magnified when difficulties arise. Specific comments included:

- The company and functional departments lack trust of the supplier's capabilities and commitment to the company.

- Functional departments do not trust supplier test data without running their own tests.

- Engineers have no confidence in the supplier's ability to meet the requirements.

- Companies have been burned by a lack of commitment when conditions are actually worse than originally estimated, even when the original estimates were clearly developed in good faith.

- Suppliers do not believe the commitment the buying company has made to them and to the development effort.

Solutions to lack of confidence include improving the supplier selection process, earlier involvement of the supplier so it has a better perspective on how requirements are identified and defined, performance over time, agreed-on performance metrics, and establishment of strategic alliances with select suppliers. Specific resolutions included the following:

- Improve the supplier selection process to ensure that only the best-in-class suppliers are integrated.

- Develop strategic alliances with selected key suppliers.

- Try to build new suppliers up from the start of the relationship—preach supplier integration benefits to the supplier and within the company.

- Coordinate buyer/supplier training sessions to educate both parties about existing and new products that each produces and the potential benefits of leveraging each other's capabilities.

- Use a pilot project team to demonstrate complimentary capabilities and the benefits of integration.

- Postmortem each project, identify the good and the bad, and try to exploit the good and reduce the bad.

Ethical Conduct Concerns. It is anticipated and encouraged that both buyer and supplier establish approaches that foster learning from each other during the supplier integration process. Parties may gain insight and learn new processes, management techniques, cost systems, technologies, and market data from each other. Much of the information may be proprietary so that nondisclosure agreements are required for confidentiality. Other information that is exchanged may not be confidential but still is important in terms of competitive positioning.

Regardless of whether the information is confidential, both parties must trust that information shared between them will not be used in any way that damages the competitive position of the other. A supplier, for example, could share information with a competitor of the buying company, or become a competitor itself. Competitive positions may also be damaged when either party withholds key nonproprietary information. Specific problem statements included:

- Confidentiality is a major concern. The company does not disclose proprietary information regarding product composition, manufacturing processes, or costs that could be provided to competitors. Further, the company does not want to be party to learning from suppliers who may put us at risk of patent infringement.

- The product development organization is not always willing to turn development over to suppliers, who in some cases may be competitors.

- Research and development personnel are unwilling to be 100 percent open out of fear of disclosing proprietary technology.

- Suppliers do not trust the buying firm because of its cost focus. "Open book costing" means "open wallet" to suppliers.

Key solutions to these problems include using formal/legal contracts, developing relationships with key suppliers to build trust through positive experiences, identifying core competencies that need to be protected, and identifying key contacts and entry points to ensure a smooth flow of the required information. Specific comments included:

- Identify core competencies and only outsource involvement outside of the core competencies.

- Conduct ongoing analysis of the make-versus-buy decision process to ensure that noncritical and confidential information will not be at risk.

- Have more involvement of key people in the decision to integrate and select suppliers so that a long-term focus is maintained and so that a broader perspective of past dealings with a supplier may be tapped.

- Develop confidentiality and nondisclosure agreements with involvement from both parties' legal departments.

- Select joint projects with quick success to build trust. Build the relationship over time—experience is the only effective trust-builder.

- Identify the key contacts in all functional areas at both facilities through which direct communication is conducted.

- Introduce a corporate multitask team approach to discipline the new product development process. Use gates and stages at critical points that identify information needs versus wants.

Integrated Supply Chain Processes

Though there are many firms that have effectively integrated suppliers into NPD, most companies indicated that supplier integration was a new strategy/process for them. Thus, processes and policies were not clearly established to determine what projects the supplier should be involved in, when the supplier should be involved, the full extent of supplier involvement, or what supplier should be selected.

No Formal Supplier Integration Processes. As indicated, the supplier integration strategy has been in place for a relatively short period of time at most firms responding to our survey. Thus, processes were not established, or the processes that were established had not yet been fully implemented, tested, and proven to be effective. This leads to initial uncertainty and a lack of consistency in decision making about projects for supplier integration, at what point suppliers should be integrated even after the decision to integrate is made, and when and what kind of information to share with a supplier during development. The effect of these situations is that suppliers are integrated too late or for the wrong reasons, so that the resulting contribution is minimized. Specific problem statements were the following:

- There is a lack of experience and expertise as government regulations only recently allowed integration of suppliers into NPD.

- There are inconsistent techniques on when and how to solicit support and participation by suppliers.

- There is a lack of a well-defined and disciplined process for integrating a supplier into new product development. Integration now depends almost entirely on technical staff and the extent they believe they can be helped by the supplier.

- The current supplier integration process is too complex and difficult to implement. Initial efforts tended to focus on trivial rather than substantive issues.

- Suppliers are selected after technical specifications are defined and the design has actually started due to the current process (or lack thereof) so that significant benefits from supplier integration are not realized.

Solutions involved either reengineering the process or developing a pilot of the process while allowing flexibility to learn and adapt the process as the new product development pilot project was implemented. Establishing clear role definitions for all functions, a more strategic role for procurement personnel, and milestones for achieving required supplier participation were the more common tactics. Specific problem resolution statements included:

- Benchmark best practices, and develop/redesign the product development process to one that will more clearly identify the role of suppliers and functional departments.

- Create a milestone at the very beginning of a product development where purchasing and research and development nominate potential suppliers as the result of a concept competition.

- Integrate supplier considerations and decision points into the new product/process development process. For example, supplier involvement may be optional in the concept phase but mandatory in the development phase.

- Include purchasing in all phases of NPD. Assign purchasing personnel full time to new product teams to be fully responsible for the procurement function for the new product.

- Use life-cycle product and process mapping to identify opportunities for continuous improvement and supplier integration opportunities.

- Focus the process on key issues—do not micromanage the process.

- Obtain total executive management support to alleviate numerous support and buy-in problems.

- Use continued influence of a dedicated procurement technical organization to drive supplier integration earlier in the NPD process.

- Provide training to all engineers, and establish appropriate measures to ensure the proper timing for supplier integration.

Ineffective Supplier Selection. The supplier selection process for supplier integration at the new product development phase, which may be significantly different from the supplier selection process for ongoing production after product introduction, was an often-reported problem. Two highly related and perhaps interdependent problems emerged from the responses. The first was an inefficient supplier selection process. The second problem was not having capable full-service suppliers from which to choose. This does not always mean that a supplier does not exist that can meet the buyer's needs. Rather, the problem may be that the buying company does not know what it needs or what capabilities suppliers possess. Specific responses to each issue are discussed below.

Ineffective Supplier Selection Process.

- It is not clear which criteria are most important for selecting full-service suppliers.

- When integrating suppliers, the company needs to choose the best one from the worldwide base. However, there is not enough staff skilled in international business and supplier evaluation processes. Therefore, domestic suppliers are typically selected for integration.

- Personal relationships played too great a role in supplier selection, or the supplier was selected by an executive.

Solutions to Ineffective Supplier Selection Process.

- Differentiate the full-service supplier selection process from the order-fulfillment supplier selection process by including such criteria as innovativeness, money spent on research and development, number of patents, design system compatibility, and so on.

- Have core design team weight the relative importance of project-specific selection criteria.

- Establish international purchasing offices in selected locations throughout the world to access updated information of world-class suppliers. Also, use a special management system that dispatches staff personnel abroad to study international purchasing business.

- Use a blind cross-functional selection process that requires team consensus.

Lack of Capable Suppliers.

- Often need to buy the most current technology with no track record of the supplier's performance. That is, the design team asks for product capabilities that may not be readily available from suppliers.

- Determining how to pick the right supplier prior to truly understanding what is needed and what is feasible is a lost cause.

- Very few suppliers have the design capability needed to meet engineering requirements and performance targets. The company spends too much time and resources developing suppliers.

- It is difficult to gain buy-in for reducing the supplier base to a manageable number of suppliers that may be effectively integrated into NPD efforts. There are far too many suppliers that may or may not have the needed capabilities for targeted commodities.

Solutions to Lack of Capable Suppliers.

- Conduct quarterly technology-sharing seminars that highlight suppliers' capabilities to ensure that the company stays abreast of new technology developments and supplier capabilities.

- Use a supplier quality improvement committee to develop suppliers to a preferred level.

- Assign qualified technical persons to the purchasing function so that their experience and technical knowledge can be used to better predict technology trends and identify capable suppliers.

- Establish earlier involvement with suppliers (for example, sharing technology road maps) to better address company needs and to access supplier technical abilities.

- Continuously evaluate active projects and postmortem completed projects to learn which suppliers are capable of long-term contributions and to identify ways to develop suppliers for the future.

- Establish supplier partners that can anticipate and exceed customer expectations.

- See the solutions to the ineffective supplier selection process as well.

Management Commitment

Management commitment by both buyer and supplier is a critical success factor for successful supplier integration. According to respondents, management commitment is critical to ensure company-to-company alignment and development of trust and to provide the necessary budgets and other resources required to achieve program goals.

Lack of management commitment may lead to frequent personnel changes during the development process that can disrupt trust and destroy learning. The lack of management commitment reinforces the lack of confidence in performance and other relational issues discussed previously. Specific problem statements included:

- Management simply will not make the commitment to work closely with the supplier.

- Management will not commit the required funds and personnel to meet aggressive targets.

- Overall, new programs are not properly staffed until the program schedule is in jeopardy. This staffing issue applies mostly to engineering and quality departments, and to a lesser extent to the materials organization. One of the results is that insufficient time is spent working with suppliers up-front, before the hardware production begins. Suppliers' issues and concerns are not addressed quickly enough, and their process improvement and cost reduction suggestions are not adequately investigated. This means higher recurring costs, an increased number of problems in test, and increased engineering change activity.

- Suppliers either do not have or do not commit the necessary resources.

- Due to frequent changes in personnel between the different business units at the company, there has not been a good flow of lessons learned from buyer to buyer and from project engineer to project engineer. This applies not only to those lessons learned on individual components, but also in the up-front supplier selection.

Solutions to these problems focused on establishing ongoing communication between managers, better detailing and estimating the required budgets and potential benefits of supplier integration, jointly committing resources, and agreeing to performance objectives and metrics. Specific responses included:

- Conduct regular top management meetings between companies to maintain communication and focus.

- Set up special budgets within product development efforts to support supplier integration activities.

- Ensure that every business unit has a sponsor (top management personnel) on the supplier management council.

- Develop more consistently accurate forecasts for the cost and time of development, so that when management is told how many dollars and people are needed they have reason to believe the estimate.

- Ensure that NPD teams are more vocal in expressing resource requirements early in a program. Have them document and back up their resource requests.

- Use a resource allocation team to calculate the effect of supplier integration on company resources.

- Assign one individual from engineering to coordinate all new program development of complex, supplier-designed system components. A purchasing representative may also be assigned. Such change should go a long way to retain and flow down lessons learned across programs.

OPERATIONAL BARRIERS

The strategic issues discussed above clearly focus on long-term and broad-based issues that set the foundation for supplier integration efforts. The operational issues discussed below are more project-specific and may arise even if the best plans are in place.

Program/Project Goal Alignment

Key to the success of supplier integration is a mutual understanding of the contribution each party makes to the success of the new product development effort and benefits received. Both parties should agree on business and technical objectives prior to the actual design and development to eliminate confusion about roles and responsibilities and to allow all parties to focus on meeting customer requirements and maximizing returns. Aligning goals and defining roles/responsibilities early in the relationship are challenging but critical processes. While a strategic supplier integration plan will provide guidelines for defining requirements and identifying roles and responsibilities, each NPD effort is unique and requires case-specific agreements.

No Goal Alignment. Setting common goals and objectives for product development is made problematic by a lack of trust and communication and by the need to prioritize potentially conflicting goals within each party's business unit. Specific problem statements regarding goal alignment are the following:

- We cannot convince suppliers or have them commit to program or project specific plans.

- Suppliers do not acknowledge the company's business needs.

- We cannot maintain alignment of objectives, especially when times get tough.

- There is a lack of focus on continuous improvement.

- It is difficult to prioritize multiple projects with each specific supplier.

- It is difficult to find the opportunity of common interest shared by integrated suppliers and the buying company.

- It has been difficult to set a common agenda or agreement between the buyer and supplier on projects or areas for joint development.

- There is an inability to focus on clear business targets as to cost, volume forecast, and timing. The buying company is always moving the bar on all of these.

Respondents identified a variety of solutions to the goal alignment problem. The majority of suggestions focused on sharing technical objectives or road maps prior to a specific development effort, establishing open lines of communication early in the development effort, and providing incentives to suppliers to align their business and technical objectives with the buyer. Specifics included:

- Develop product road maps and a technology management strategy to be shared with suppliers so that project-specific goals are aligned in advance of specific NPD efforts.

- Communicate within the organization that supplier integration decisions are not to be made solely by technical development staff.

- Establish the project manager's roles and responsibilities earlier.

- Define a common agenda. Work together with the supplier to set goals and objectives and define mutual benefits.

- Conduct monthly project priority reviews with each supplier.

- Develop in advance alternatives for critical components or systems, and plan for market contingencies.

- Limit the number of continuous improvement and supplier integration initiatives to several, so that all parties agree about what is important for success.

- Increase expectations from supplier leveraging but provide greater rewards (such as more volume and profit).

Ill-defined Roles and Responsibilities. Closely related to the goal alignment problem is the challenge of clearly defining the roles and responsibilities of each party at different stages in the NPD process. Although each party may agree about why they have entered into the codevelopment effort and what the desired outcomes are, many companies stated that it is difficult to define and divide actual responsibilities because of culture, lack of planning and process, and ambiguous or poorly communicated customer requirements. Specific problems are as follows:

- Establishing a clear division of program management responsibilities between OEM and supplier is complicated. Understanding each other's roles is a major issue.

- Cultural attitude towards integration leads to conflicts about who's in charge.

- When problems come up, both the buyer and suppliers tend to initially point fingers at each other, not acknowledging joint responsibility.

- Clear definition of what had been developed individually by each party prior to integration and agreement, versus what was jointly developed after the agreement had been executed, is often problematic.

- The supplier does not understand total system requirements.

- The buyer cannot clearly communicate project objectives and keep the supplier up to speed when objectives or timelines change.

- It is difficult to establish a common language between buyer and supplier. For example, if the company needs to develop a sensitive skin product but does not define what *sensitive skin* means in terms of performance attributes required, suppliers may lack direction and purpose. Suppliers used to try to meet the specifications although they had no idea of the overall product mission.

Solutions to this type of problem included creating smaller and more focused teams to control the process, formally defining requirements early in the process, assigning actual names to responsibilities, and establishing common terms to reduce ambiguity. Specific solutions are the following:

- Use smaller teams with more clearly defined leadership and roles. Ensure that actual names are assigned to responsibilities rather than just assigning a functional department.

- Increase supplier design responsibility, and let the supplier be more creative.

- Develop and document a product assurance plan that defines roles and responsibilities. Perhaps integrate the plan into internal ISO 9000 efforts.

- Better define or benchmark each other's product development capabilities prior to any codevelopment activities. Also, clearly establish ownership rights of jointly developed products that were either required or funded for the product development.

- Send product criteria for success and project briefs to each respective supplier. Ensure that these briefs are in the hands of suppliers prior to the start of any development.

- Conduct a comprehensive quality function deployment (QFD) exercise with cross-functional teams from both firms. This will help people who have worked together establish a clear mutual language and true understanding of required attributes for the first time.

"Intrusive" Customer Involvement. Some respondents identified their customer's involvement in the product development process as causing problems. These included the customer's requirement to approve all design changes, which caused delays in the project and dictating a portion of the design without considering alternatives. The companies dealt with these challenges by ensuring that the customer was continuously involved in the development process to reduce approval bottlenecks, having marketing work closer with the customer by fully reviewing the customer requirements as well as what competitors offer, and working more closely with the customer to define the system requirements early in the process.

Honest and Effective Communication

Direct and open communication at all levels and functions of both parties' organization has repeatedly been identified as a critical success factor for supplier integration. Verbal and electronic communication allow the parties to align goals, share technical and business information, and solve problems in a timely manner. However, each mode of communication is challenging in its own respects.

Verbal Communication Problems. The main concerns with verbal communication included lack of candor, frequency, timeliness, and effectiveness. Companies reported the following specific problems:

- Achieving open and honest communication among the various suppliers integrated into the project is difficult.

- Better and more complete communication is needed throughout the process.

- Face-to-face communication is critical during supplier integration, but the use of worldwide suppliers makes such communication on a regular basis costly and impractical.

Solutions included increased use of colocation of personnel, trust-building through training and management commitment, and electronic communication. Specific solutions included:

- To instill trust between and within each firm and to foster communication, involve senior management prior to formalizing the agreement to integrate.

- Use functional and supplier colocation processes to encourage communication. Realize that colocation may be appropriate throughout the NPD process or just for selected stages, such as concept development or product testing.

- Put suppliers on the core NPD project team when appropriate, and make more extensive use of team meetings.

- Establish a strong supplier interface by assigning formal responsibility with one person at both companies to be the integration champion or ombudsman.

- Increase cyberspace communication with suppliers, including fully integrated EDI and videoconferencing.

Electronic Communication Issues. Electronic communication is often used in supplier integration efforts to share technical information such as drawings and specifications. It also is frequently used for nontechnical information-sharing when verbal communication is neither required nor practical. The main electronic communication problem is system compatibility between the buyer and supplier. Specific problems include the following:

- It is difficult to integrate suppliers into our systems and to develop compatible systems.

- There is a lack of complete deployment of product and process design hardware/software.

- Transfer of technical design data is difficult due to incompatible or nonexistent supplier systems.

Solutions to the system incompatibility problem focused on greater use of the Internet, using system compatibility as a supplier selection criterion, and helping suppliers develop their systems. Specific approaches are as follows:

- Make greater use of the Internet to minimize systems compatibility problems.

- Provide technical support and perhaps favorable funding for selected suppliers to develop compatible design systems.

- Hire a third party to coordinate design and information system compatibility.

- Add system performance/compatibility to supplier rating criteria.

- Conduct supplier alliance meetings to pursue/share/resolve system issues.

- Give the supplier more direct access to systems and access to information over the World Wide Web.

- Continue to aggressively implement electronic commerce capabilities internally, while working directly with the supply chain to assist them in developing and implementing capabilities.

- Work with industry groups (customers, OEMs, suppliers) to develop or direct future industry standards for electronic communication and design systems.

Integration Problems

Many respondents indicated that getting people with different professional backgrounds to work together within their own business unit is a challenge in itself, so that integrating suppliers into NPD was practically impossible. Even with internal cross-functional participation and decision making, however, supplier integration is complicated by many of the problems discussed earlier. By addressing the problems identified earlier, many of the actual integration problems discussed in the following sections may be proactively mitigated. However, people with different personalities and interests must still implement the process, so problems may still occur. Major issues are as follows.

No Internal Cross-functional Integration. Although total quality management and related processes such as concurrent engineering have been adopted in many industries, many companies still report problems with cross-functional team integration within their business unit. The majority of problems focused on engineering's reluctance to involve other functional departments in decision-making (similar to the not-invented-here syndrome). Specific problems are as follows:

- Engineering does not involve purchasing soon enough in the project. However, purchasing knows the best suppliers to use for most projects—the engineer does not.

- Integration across design disciplines is uncertain. Very strong technical groups are not good at integrating other functions into their work. Consequently, the company may optimize the process cycle, but have only a limited selection of poor-efficiency machinery to choose from because of lack of other functional involvement.

- Supply management does not have the ability to be aware of all NPD activities in such a diverse corporation.

- Having purchasing's role and responsibility well defined and bought into as a primary role in supplier management is difficult.

- There is fragmented purchasing and companywide unwillingness to collaborate. This is complicated by not having appropriate computer-based systems to identify the appropriate opportunities.

Solutions to these challenges focus on reengineering the organization and processes to facilitate cross-functional integration, developing a minimal competency across functions in nontechnical activities to better understand business requirements and opportunities, and gaining top management support for cross-functional activities. Specific solutions were the following:

- Gain support from executive management, and solicit their involvement to drive cross-functional integration.

- Reorganize the company structure to support the concept of platform teams. All the major functions are members of the product platform team, including purchasing.

- Install within the engineering department several experienced developmental buyers whose primary duty is to interface with engineering and suppliers on new products.

- Better communicate the benefits of cross-functional teams.

- Physically integrate working parties so that more people share common work space.

- Establish close linkage with engineering management so that supply management is aware of and participating in major NPD initiatives early.

- Implement the SAP R3 software suite to provide real-time database and analysis tools across all functional areas.

- Use job-rotation to develop a breadth of technical and business skills in selected employees.

Supplier Integration Challenges. The supplier integration problems discussed in this section focus on the difficulty of coordinating the efforts of partners willing to collaborate, rather than on getting both parties to agree to collaborate. The main causes of this type of problem are physical location and potentially integrating too many suppliers, as discussed below:

- Physical distance between the buying company and suppliers cause communication problems and project delays.

- Key supplier personnel are not in close proximity to our development center. This makes communication difficult.

- There are too many suppliers to be effectively integrated into NPD.

Companies indicate that colocation and electronic communication can be used effectively to better coordinate new product development efforts with suppliers. Further, by limiting the number of supplier integration efforts to a few key projects, limited resources can be effectively focused on managing those efforts. Specific solutions are as follows:

- Ensure that the company has established a supplier integration strategy, and follow that strategy.

- Better define the integrated supplier relationship and responsibilities.

- Make greater use of colocation.

- Establish a liaison office in regional markets to assist with supplier integration into NPD issues.

- Support improvement of the information system. Develop cross-country electronic communication with all key suppliers to support supplier integration efforts.

- Solutions of communication problems help resolve many of the supplier integration problems as well.

Meeting Customer Requirements. Respondents indicated that even with apparently smooth supplier integration and new product development efforts, increasingly-demanding customer requirements are difficult to realize. All of the up-front planning required to determine whether supplier integration is needed, when it is needed, which supplier is needed, and so on leads to potential time delays that would be unacceptable to the ultimate customer.

The intensity of these problems may be industry-specific. In a time-to-market environment in which customers are willing to accept some minor problems with the product in order to maintain leading-edge capabilities and in which product upgrades are relatively easy to implement, such as the personal computer software market, these barriers may be intense. In time-to-zero-defect volume production environments, where the long-term quality and reliability of the product is critical and product failures and modifications are costly, these problems may be less intense. That is, supplier integration into a concurrent engineering process may extend the time needed to develop product concepts and to draft business and technical requirements. However, it may also shorten the actual design, test, and ramp-up to zero-defect volume production phases so that *overall* cycle time (from concept to customer) is shorter with supplier integration.

Even in time-to-market environments, however, the unacceptable time required to integrate suppliers may reflect more on poor internal strategies and processes (such as ineffective supplier selection or lack of supplier integration strategy) than on supplier integration per se. Regardless, specific problems reported were these:

- There is insufficient time to involve a large number of suppliers simultaneously and still meet product launch dates.

- Delivery dates must be met. Supplier integration potentially makes meeting delivery mandates difficult.

- Time involved in team formation leads to delays.

- Speed to market is simply not quick enough with supplier integration.

Keys to ensuring that customer requirements are met in a timely fashion when integrating suppliers include integrating only critical suppliers, identifying and agreeing on program objectives early in the process, establishing main contacts at all facilities responsible for communication of requirements and status information, and making greater use of electronic communication. Specific solutions are discussed below:

- Limit full integration to a few key suppliers on a given program.

- Form a cross-functional team with purchasing, engineering, quality, manufacturing, the customer, and the supplier to develop a strategic plan (with responsibility, milestones, and budget identified) for each new major program.

- Establish buyer and supplier technical offices to provide real-time technical feedback and a communication link.

- Conduct ongoing product meetings with suppliers to keep them as up-to-date as possible on all program requirements.

- Establish accurate and reliable lead times in order to arrange different priorities.

- Develop better scheduling criteria and realistic project dates, especially during revisions.

Competitive Concerns

The following section discusses a number of competitive concerns that may arise when integrating suppliers into new product development efforts.

Price Pressures. Many respondents indicated that it is difficult to maintain a sense of competitive pressure on an integrated supplier to ensure that the supplier is charging a fair price for products and services. The close relationship in an integration effort generally requires trust that each party is approaching the effort from a win-win perspective. However, it is clear from the responses that many companies feel that it may be necessary to create competitive market pressures as a check on the trusting relationship. This seems to be especially true when problems arise or changes are made to the original agreement. Specific concerns were the following:

- There exists a great fear in the marketplace that if you trust too much you are going to be taken advantage of on price.

- Buyers are afraid to lock into a long-term relationship with suppliers and give up competitive pressure.

- There is concern about price paid. That is, some companies do not feel comfortable with the competitiveness of integrated suppliers versus the traditional arm's length negotiation process.

- Coengineering made the discussion on cost difficult because every concept change will result in a request for a price change.

Solutions to this problem focused on developing a better understanding of each other's cost system, educating final external customers about the strategic benefits of supplier integration (such as innovation, quality, and systematic price reduction), and developing agreements on how to handle technical and market-induced price changes early in the process. Specific solutions are as follows:

- Continue benchmarking the industry, and communicate results in an effort to keep suppliers competitive.

- Meet with the supplier's cost accountant to determine the supplier's view of cost.

- Periodically apply internally developed market price and total cost of ownership models to test the relationship's value.

- Develop an agreement that allows for price changes due to market changes. Use target costing and what-if analysis to plan for contingencies.

- Hone pricing in alliance agreements to prove to clients that pricing is at least as good as—if not better than—the pricing available without supplier integration.

- Bring testimonials where partnerships provided actual cash returns above what could be expected without supplier integration.

Risk and Reward Sharing. Many respondents indicated that suppliers are more than willing to share in the benefits of supplier integration, but have a less clear understanding and willingness to share the risks of new product development efforts. Further, respondents indicated that getting supplier buy-in to the process without a guaranteed long-term sole-source production contract is challenging. Specific problems are as follows:

- Our products are subject to major competition and customer price erosion. We also are a global company with 41 operations worldwide. Products in the development stage must have the best production pricing when going to market. Contract negotiations must have clauses to renegotiate the "me too" and customer demands for lower prices.

- Suppliers are capable of defining and accepting reward targets, but less comfortable with managing risk.

- It is hard to find suppliers who are willing to provide development-only services and forego manufacturing the product.

- Rapid change in product mix and numerous dropped products places a strain on some supplier relationships.

- It is difficult to fully reward the supplier for time and expenses incurred to develop new products and at the same time reduce our costs for new product.

- It is hard to come to agreement on fair share of joint development gains. Before trust is developed, this negotiation is difficult for the parties.

- It is difficult to persuade suppliers to participate without making long-term sole-source commitments to them, which would impede competition in a changing marketplace at a later date.

Solutions to these problems focus on negotiating terms and conditions early in the process, keeping one's own commitments, developing target-cost designs, identifying the minimum production volume required for the supplier to realize a fair return on its investment, and offering the integrated supplier special opportunities to match market level prices before awarding new production contracts. Specific recommendations are listed below:

- Work with suppliers to understand and model risks, and find ways to minimize or eliminate risks before start-up of the integrated team.

- Develop a formal strategic negotiating plan with total goals and objectives defined by a cross-functional team that is used in the concept development and supplier selection phases of new product development. Negotiating sessions are led by the purchasing function, with backup by the total team.

- Develop a memo of understandings at beginning of program that addresses alternative courses of action in the case of market-induced, buyer-induced, or supplier-induced changes.

- Establish a set time to recoup development costs based on open-book cost sharing information. Also, offer the integrated supplier the first right to match price on a competitor initiative after the integrated supplier's initial production contract is completed.

- Clearly communicate project requirements up-front to prevent misunderstandings.

- Consolidate suppliers involved in product development to ensure that work is available on some projects if others are dropped.

- Minimize supplier risk by assisting the supplier in preliminary financing and production planning.

- Keep your own commitments.

Design Standardization. Standardization of designs and processes has been effectively used to improve product quality, reduce cycle times, and lower costs of new product development efforts. Three respondents indicated that the lack of standardization has created a barrier to successful supplier integration.

- Inability to standardize is a significant supplier integration barrier. Our roots are as an engineering company; hence, people have been rewarded and our culture revolves around constant change and improvement. This sounds like a good idea, but it destroys any ability to do things once and move on. We are always changing our specifications and even our standards.

- No easy-to-use preferred supply/component database is accessible to design. Manual communications (such as a paper database with no search engine) are too cumbersome to use. As a result, each design organization reinvents the wheel.

- It is difficult to change the paradigm of how our engineering staff and the supplier work together. It is particularly important that we standardize the design of the units we purchase to make the integration process effective.

Solutions for the above problems include:

- Change from a project-focused organization to a product-focused organization.
- Develop standard components using supplier, industry, and internal inputs from which to build and economize new designs.
- Make the review of all preferred components/suppliers available to all internal functions on an intranet.
- Have engineers spend time with the people on the supplier's assembly line. By seeing the effect of a nonstandard design on the supply chain firsthand, engineers realize the importance of standardizing.

CONCLUSION

Interrelated strategic and operational barriers create significant challenges for successful supplier integration. Only by developing an organizational plan and structure to support supplier integration will the long-term benefits of supplier integration be achieved.

The primary tasks for an effective supplier integration strategy are

- Definition and nurturing of core competencies
- Communication internally and to the supply base of the company's product differentiation strategy
- Redesign of the NPD process based on best-in-class performance
- Formalizing, through executive policy, the process and requirements for supplier integration (or requirements for detailed explanation of why supplier integration would not be pursued) for all NPD efforts.
- Enhancing supply-base capabilities by identifying, developing, and selecting the best-in-class suppliers
- Managing the process

A top-down management approach is required to drive internal and supply chain support and enthusiasm for supplier integration into NPD. Barriers are most significant for initial start firms that have not developed a long-term strategic plan for supplier integration. Many of the barriers truly relate to changing paradigms, lack of correct organization structure, and lack of process or role definition. Strategic and operational barriers are highly interrelated and likely are interdependent, so that a solution for one barrier may go a long way in mitigating many other barriers.

Key processes or strategies that were reported to solutions for a wide variety of strategic and operational problems included:

- Share technology and business road maps (2, 5, and 10 year projections) to align cross-enterprise objectives and to secure long-term sources of innovation.

- Develop formal guidelines that can be adapted to specific supplier integration efforts and that identify the who, what, where, when, why, and how of supplier integration.

- Start with several small-scale sure-win integration efforts to build momentum for change and the integration strategy.

- Use colocation strategically—it is not a panacea.

- Jointly develop—or at least jointly review and agree on—all business and technical requirements and metrics.

- Use confidentiality and nondisclosure agreements even when a high level of trust exists. Personnel may change, making handshake agreements hard to enforce.

- Assign an integration champion at both firms to drive and manage integration efforts.

By proactively addressing the interrelated strategic and operational barriers, a company positions itself for gaining significant competitive advantages from supplier integration both in the long- and short-term. Though it is difficult to do so, the proactive company provides a foundation for a clear path to NPD success. Without proactively addressing these issues, a company will pick away at strategic issues while balancing operational pressures and interests on its way to suboptimal short-term performance without ever realizing any long-term benefits.

Chapter 10
Summary and Conclusion

Integration of suppliers into new product development efforts is a strategy that allows a company to leverage the expertise and capabilities of its supply base to achieve a competitive advantage in an increasingly demanding market environment. In Chapter 1, we described some of the typical "hard" results of supplier integration into new product development, in terms of percentage improvements in cost, quality, and so on. The companies we studied also reported achieving important "soft" results due to their supplier integration efforts.

- 85.2 percent of the companies reported achieving a better design/technology in their finished product or service.

- 83.5 percent reported achieving a better design of the purchased item.

- 76.2 percent reported a smoother ramp-up to volume production due to the supplier's involvement.

- 75.4 percent reported a design that was easier for the supplier to execute

- 73.8 percent reported a design that was less costly for the supplier to execute.

- 68.6 percent of the companies reported that because of their supplier integration efforts, they are better positioned to access new technologies for future new product developments.

While the results of successful supplier integration efforts are impressive, we also found a wide range of outcomes in the companies we examined. Success is by no means automatic. We identified three general requirements that are key to making supplier integration into new product development successful. They are

- A new product development process engineered to facilitate supplier involvement. The new product development process should create the organizational infrastructure to manage a complex set of cross-functional and cross-organizational relationships during new product development. This requires

  —A clear linkage between the NPD process and the company's strategic objectives

—A well-defined NPD process that is understood by all involved parties and that clearly lays out responsibilities and expectations of all parties (including suppliers) in the process

—A clearly defined role, early in the process, for the procurement function and for select suppliers

- A strategic planning process for supplier integration into new product development. In order to make a real contribution to competitive advantage, supplier integration must be a part of the company's strategy, not an ad hoc tactic applied haphazardly. The strategic planning process should include formal steps to

—Identify current and future needs for technologies and capabilities from external sources

—Develop and maintain a world-class supply base whose culture, capabilities, and strategic objectives are well-aligned with the company's

—Develop a bookshelf of viable new technologies and suppliers of those technologies to meet future needs

- An effective execution process for supplier integration. Once supplier integration is adopted as a strategy and suppliers are selected for a particular NPD project, their involvement must be managed on a day-to-day basis. Key considerations in maximizing the supplier's impact include giving the supplier an active role on the project team, involving the supplier in establishing metrics and targets for the project, extensive communication and information sharing with the supplier, and direct involvement of suppliers in decision making and problem solving during the NPD project.

Descriptions and case examples of successful strategies for dealing with these general requirements have been described in Chapters 3 through 8, but there is no single right way to manage supplier integration into new product development. Based on our work with the companies that participated in this study, however, we know something about what leads to success. Is *your* company ready to leverage its supply base to improve new product development efforts? Consider the following issues:

- Have you assessed existing capabilities and competencies and compared them to future new product/process/service requirements?

- Do you have a structured process encouraging use of existing or industry standard materials, processes, components, services, and so on before establishing unique or custom requirements in a new product, process, or service?

- Do you use cross-functional teams and specific, well-defined supplier selection criteria to proactively identify and select suppliers for NPD efforts?

- In assessing and selecting suppliers, do you pay significant attention to the fit of the supplier's capabilities and competencies with your current and future requirements?

- Do you have a formal process for determining the need for supplier input (both timing and extent of input) in your new product/process/service development efforts?

- Do you employ cross-functional, cross-organizational teams (including suppliers) to work on new product/process/service development?

- Do you use colocation and/or regular scheduled meetings among procurement, supplier, and all other personnel to facilitate communications during the NPD process?

- Do your NPD teams establish clear and specific business and technical objectives (including timetables) for NPD projects?

- Do you establish and agree on business and technical objectives for NPD projects with your suppliers?

- Do you have clear metrics for evaluating the success of NPD projects?

- Do you regularly review NPD-related capability and competency requirements with suppliers?

- Do you regularly and openly share information regarding customer requirements, technology, and cost with suppliers involved in NPD efforts?

There are significant barriers to integrating suppliers into new product development, but these barriers can be overcome. There are many encouraging success stories. Companies that have carefully planned and managed their attempts at supplier integration have realized impressive results. As increasing demands for lower costs, higher quality, and shorter cycle times drive companies to rely more on outside suppliers for production and delivery of products, companies cannot afford to overlook the potential benefits of leveraging the supply base in the new product development arena as well.

Appendix A
Additional Readings

Bidault, Christina, Francis Despres, and Charles Butler (1998). "New Product Development and Early Supplier Involvement (ESI): The Drivers of ESI Adoption," *International Journal of Technology Management,* 15: 1, 2, pp. 49–69.

Bidault, Christina, Francis Despres, and Charles Butler (April 1998). "The Drivers of Cooperation Between Buyers and Suppliers for Product Innovation," *Research Policy,* 26: 7, 8, pp. 719–732.

Birou, Laura M. (1994). *The Role of the Buyer-Supplier Linkage in an Integrated Product Development Environment,* a doctoral dissertation. East Lansing, MI: Michigan State University.

Bozdogan, Kirkor, John Deyst, David Hoult, and Malee Lucas (July 1998). "Architectural Innovation in Product Development Through Early Supplier Integration," *R & D Management,* 28: 3, pp. 163–173.

Chamberlain, Gary (May 18, 1998). "Teamwork Gives Maytag a Jump on Competition," *Design News,* 53: 10, pp. S13–S18.

Culley, Stephen J., Oliver P. Boston, and Christopher A. McMahon (1999). "Suppliers in New Product Development: Their Information and Integration," *Journal of Engineering Design,* 10: 1, pp. 59–75.

Curtis, Christine (March 3, 1997). "E-Commerce Among Businesses Can Improve the Bottom Line," *Communications Week,* 652: Opinion, p. 37.

Dietz, Dan (March 1995). "An Infrastructure for Integration," *Mechanical Engineering,* 117: 3, pp. 78–80.

Fish, Rick (November 1994). "Appliance Manufacturers Asking More of Parts, Material Suppliers," *Modern Plastics,* 71: 11, p. 108.

Forrest, David (May 25, 1994). "Quick Response Brings Retailers Up to Speed," *Computing Canada,* 20: 11, p. 23.

Fruin, W. Mark (August 1998). "Smart Cards and Product-Development Strategies in the Electronics Industry in Japan," *IEEE Transactions on Engineering Management,* 45: 3, pp. 241–249.

Laage-Hellman, Jens (1997). *Business Networks in Japan: Supplier-Customer Interaction in Product Development.* London: Routledge.

Laseter, Timothy M. (1998). *Balanced Sourcing: Cooperation and Competition in Supplier Relationships*. San Francisco, CA: Jossey-Bass Publishers.

"NSF Bankrolls Leading-Edge Research," *Purchasing*, 118: 2 (February 16, 1995), pp. 23–24.

Prasad, Biren (July/August 1997). "Sharing Responsibilities with Suppliers in a Concurrent Engineering Organization," *Industrial Management*, 39: 4, pp. 5–6.

Quint, Barbara (March 1995). "Internet Content-Finally," *Information Today*, 12: 3, pp. 7–9.

Ragatz, Gary L., Robert B. Handfield, Thomas V. Scannell (1997). "Success Factors for Integrating Suppliers into New Product Development," *The Journal of Product Innovation Management*, 14: 3, pp. 190–202.

von Hippel, Eric (May 1998). "Economics of Product Development by Users: The Impact of 'Sticky' Local Information," *Management Science*, 44: 5, pp. 629–644.

Index